The
Blue
Streak

The Blue Streak

some observations, mostly about advertising,

by
Fairfax M. Cone

Crain
Communications
Inc.

Foreword

What comprises the body of this book is my personal selection of memos or bits of memos from a steady stream which Fairfax M. Cone directed to the Chicago staff of the Foote. Cone & Belding advertising agency over a period of some 22 years — from the beginning of 1948 to the end of 1969.

They were not intended to be put into a book. They are principally about advertising and business, but they occasionally wander far afield. As Cone said when he distributed the first of these blue striped memos "To the Organization" (which came to be known as The Blue Streak) on Jan. 12, 1948:

"On numerous occasions, sometimes several times a week, there is something I want to discuss with a number of people in our organization. Usually it is impossible to get everyone together at just the right moment. Sometimes there is no place to get together. And often the thing is put off until it is forgotten.

"This, then, inaugurates a series of notes by which I hope to talk to a good many of you about a large number of things— exactly when they occur to me. Some of these notes will be of interest to only a few of you . . . You will decide whether [each memorandum] belongs in your wastebasket."

From time to time one or another of these Blue Streaks has been called to my attention. They have seemed perceptive and interesting to me, holding up a mirror, as they do, to two exciting decades of the advertising business and reflecting the ideas, impressions and prejudices of a most uncommon man — one whose influence not only on advertising but on education and the civic welfare of the city of Chicago will not soon be forgotten.

I emphasize that the material in this book consists of my personal selection, comprising perhaps one-tenth of what Fax Cone actually wrote, because he and others who saw them all may not agree that those bits and pieces I have selected for inclusion here are as good or as representative as they might have been. In self defense, I submit that I have picked those I personally liked—either because of the opinions they express, the manner in which they express them, or the bits of light they shed on the forgotten lore of the years they cover. Memos covering purely internal agency matters, and many which have wandered too far afield (such as most of the descriptions of Europe which Cone sent back from an extensive trip in the '50s) have been excised. So too have many which were essentially repetitious, as is bound to be the case when a man affirms and re-affirms basic principles over a long period of years.

The task of editing this material has been a very pleasant personal one. The "Blue Streaks," sometimes written one day after the next, sometimes at relatively infrequent intervals, give an interesting insight into the character of one of advertising's soundest and most engaging practitioners—a man who not only served his own company and its clients and numerous national advertising organizations exceptionally well, but found time and energy also to serve in a host of civic and philanthropic areas, most notably as chairman of the board of trustees of the University of Chicago.

This is not a book to be read from cover to cover at one sitting, nor does it necessarily require that it be read in sequence. It is filled with wise and pungent comments on the advertising business, on life and living in general, on people and events. In addition to outlining a sharp and well defined sales and advertising philosophy, it mirrors changes in the life styles of the United States and of the world during the two postwar decades which it spans.

It will, of course, be of principal interest to people in advertising and marketing, in publishing and broadcasting. But in browsing through it, I hope any reader will see for himself why Fairfax Mastick Cone, perhaps more than any other single individual in advertising, has brightened my perspective on the business and contributed mightily to my firm conviction that advertising people are more interesting, more fun to be with and more fun to work with and write about, than almost any other group you could name.

S. R. Bernstein,
Chairman, Executive Committee,
Crain Communications Inc.

Chicago,
Feb. 19, 1973

1948

January 15

Foote, Cone & Belding has been requested by the State Department to prepare an advertising campaign on the American business system for circulation abroad.

The campaign will be offered through The Advertising Council.

(Nothing ever came of this advertising campaign abroad. Whether it was because there was no machinery like the Council's to arrange media and advertiser support for such a venture or whether the subject was deemed to be political rather than economic, I don't know. Anyway, it died aborning.

(However, the booklet that we produced to go with the advertising campaign, a lengthy argument in favor of the free-enterprise system, achieved wide circulation at home, where millions of workers received copies in their pay envelopes.)

February 3

The estimated 1947 volume for each of the advertising agencies billing $10 million or more, published last week in *Advertising Age,* puts Foote, Cone & Belding at $52 million.

This is correct.

The exact amount was $52,313,158.99 ...

Foote, Cone & Belding in its fifth year is estimated to have ranked fifth among all advertising agencies.

February 5

Looking yesterday at our telephone bill for last year got me to looking also at some other figures.

One that might seem odd for an advertising agency, was the huge one for legal services.

The total in 1947 was $117,571.

A major item: every advertisement that appears in print and every radio commercial that goes on the air for each of our clients, is submitted first for legal approval.

February 11

The November issue of *Seventeen,* for which the Starch report is just in, indicates that 38% of the girls interviewed "read most" of the more than 400 words in the Kotex full page advertisement under the headline "Are you in the know?"

That this is a figure rarely reached even by moving picture advertising makes it interesting.

However, the most interesting thing about this advertisement is that it is one of a series that is now in its fifth year, in which neither the headline nor the layout has been changed from the first insertion.

It is a campaign in which the basic idea remains continuously fresh and important simply by playing variations on the theme. It requires no change in appeal, and no change in format.

(Starch readership figures have always been moot. If your advertisement showed up well in the door-to-door sample you were inclined to award Starch biblical standing. If it was low you were apt to take a somewhat dimmer view.

(I always felt that if readership figures were applied to a campaign, or to a number of insertions of a given advertisement, the averages were probably indicative and should be heeded either as warnings or as go-ahead signals.)

February 20

Those of you who do not receive full reports from the Radio Department on advertising agency performance according to the Hooperatings of evening and Sunday afternoon programs will be interested in the latest standings.

For January, Foote, Cone & Belding (with 6 programs) ranks second, with an average rating of 17.2. J. Walter Thompson Company (7 programs) was first with 18.2; Russell M. Seeds (3) was third with 15.2; Young & Rubicam (10), fourth with 13.7; The Biow Company (5), fifth with 13.0.

Some of the others: McCann-Erickson, Inc. (3) ranked tenth with 11.0; Dancer-Fitzgerald-Sample (10), eleventh with 10.8; BBD&O (7), fourteenth with 9.6; Ruthrauff & Ryan (8), fifteenth with 9.3; N. W. Ayer & Son (4), sixteenth with 8.3.

The Hooperatings represent the percentage of telephone homes, in 36 representative cities, reported listening to the various programs according to coincidental telephone check.

(Seven of the ten most popular radio programs were comedies. Jack Benny, Fibber McGee and Molly, Bob Hope, Phil Harris, My Friend Irma, Fred Allen, Duffy's Tavern.

(Ten years later, television had altered the entertainment pattern. Seven of the top ten programs were Westerns. Gunsmoke. Wagon Train. Have Gun, Will Travel. Rifleman. Maverick. Wells Fargo. Wyatt Earp. Danny Thomas was the lone comic.)

March 1

The following are sober estimates by Frank Stanton, president of the Columbia Broadcasting System, of what may be ahead in the next 25 years of broadcasting:

"One of the interesting things about Radio is how safe it is to predict quite fantastic things about it . . . and then see them come true.

"It seems hard to believe, for example, that within the next 25 years tiny little radio sets will be carried about in one's pocket — radios no larger than a pocketwatch — yet capable of bringing you programs with almost all the quality of your present sets at home . . .

"I think you can also count on having personal sending sets to carry around in your pocket, too. You'll be able to make your own broadcasts—to tell the family you'll be late for dinner, for example.

"Different types of developments are also well on their way. With a radio device known as facsimile broadcasting, your home radio set will be able—during the small hours of the night—to print your copy of the morning newspaper, page by page, with its pictures in full color . . .

"And I have yet to mention the biggest development of all—Television—sending living sight as well as sound through the air into the nation's homes. Television is certain to become as familiar to almost everyone as Radio is today. Great networks of television stations will bring programs to you wherever you live . . ."

(Frank Stanton failed to foresee only that the majority of television programs [aside from the excellent news and special events programs] would be tasteless, meager and monotonous. And thoroughly acceptable to most viewers.

(Newest thing in television is the so-called talk show whose doubtful contribution to the medium is the airing of second and third-string entertainers who make the rounds with slightly

sanitized nightclub jokes and repartee. The live audiences who have heard it all before howl with joy to prove their sophistication—particularly when a familiar blue line is bleeped.)

March 19

The other night at an A.N.A. meeting, I was complimented by one of the members on the steady growth of this agency. When I told him the reason was that we had good clients, he seemed to find this a new idea, and later made quite a point of it.

I repeat it to you, because it is important. An advertising agency cannot be better than its clients. It may be weaker, or it may be equal, but it can't be stronger.

April 16

At a meeting of The Advertising Council yesterday in New York City, the United States Forestry Service presented The Council with a plaque in appreciation of the Forest Fire Prevention advertising campaign which, it was reported, has prevented more than 50,000 expected forest fires since the end of the war.

Interpreted in goods, the Forestry Service estimated the saving to equal 1,500,000 tons of newsprint—plus 45,000 five-room frame houses.

The campaign, since its inception, has been the work of Foote, Cone & Belding in Los Angeles.

(This is now the Council's oldest campaign; still produced by Foote, Cone & Belding in Los Angeles.)

April 29

On confidence in advertising.

I think it is the reason why "WHY" headlines usually develop compelling copy. You can't tell why anyone should want a product unless you can really prove why.

"SEE" is another confident beginning. So is "NOW". So is "HOW".

Headlines in the form of questions frequently build confidence quickly. Cellucotton's "Are you in the know?" is a classic example.

The thing is, in advertising, as everywhere else, confidence in the giver is all that makes a promise any good.

May 18

There is an unusual advertising campaign for Schenley

Cream of Kentucky whiskey that broke in newspapers all over the country last week.

I think it is pretty good advertising.

But the most extraordinary thing about this campaign, which features face analysis based around drawings by Norman Rockwell, is that it was developed for Cream of Kentucky by Lord & Thomas in the middle 1930s, and appeared right up to the time Cream of Kentucky was taken off the market when war rationing began.

It now is repeated without change.

Not even seven years can dull a good idea.

May 26

Twelve accounts which we have declined at one time or another during the past several years, billed more than $4 million *in newspapers alone* in 1947, according to Media Records as reported in *Printers' Ink* for May 21.

I point this out simply because I wouldn't change my vote on any one of these today. Ten are neither leaders nor potential leaders—which is something every client that we work for is . . . and always must be.

June 7

A little while ago, Gen. B. M. Fitch, U. S. Army, Chief of Military Personnel Procurement, asked Mr. Charles G. Mortimer, Jr. of General Foods, to give him a yardstick by which the Army could choose an advertising agency. Mr. Mortimer's reply appears below in full, for I believe that in it he has outlined the perfect relationship between advertiser and agency:

"My dear General Fitch:

"You have asked us to give you the benefit of our experience in the selection of an advertising agency and in the maintenance of most effective relationships with an agency.

"While I could not give specific advice on these matters as related to your problem—not knowing enough about it—I can point out certain principles which evolved from our long working experience with agencies.

"When we select an agency we consider that we are selecting a working partner for a very long period of time and we approach the job just as carefully and objectively as possible.

"Because our product accounts are usually sizable ones, we feel that we must have very complete service. Our agencies must be fully equipped to handle all types of media including the very complex business of radio production. Our agencies must be able to give us nation-wide service, which entails having more than one production location. They must be equipped to give extensive market research — and this entails adequate personnel for field operations. The selling and advertising plans underlying the most effective spending of a million or more dollars must be based on very substantial data and this requires a lot of footwork—intensive study of various sections of the country, population and age groups, public attitudes, etc. Usually such extensive services can be afforded only by the larger advertising agencies. When we select an agency we do not invite all agencies to solicit us. We make up a list of those agencies which we feel could qualify on the basis of facilities, established reputation for good work, integrity and stability, and invite only those to solicit the business.

"We make agency selections very infrequently. One of our three agencies has served us since General Foods was established; the second, since 1929; the third, appointed in 1945, we hope to work with equally long.

"We feel that frequent changes in agencies would result in incalculable losses in experience and in service. What you buy in an agency is simply service—the service of knowledge and experience, talent and integrity in people. It takes agency personnel a long time to deeply understand the problem, to accumulate the necessary factual data. This is a period of mutual investment, the yield of which comes later. With frequent change this investment period is simply repeated with the real pay-off in effectiveness greatly diminished.

"Furthermore, having selected our agencies carefully, we let them know that as long as the service given us comes up to highest standards of effectiveness and disinterestedness, they are not in danger of losing the account. They are not threatened with divorce without grounds, in short. We want them to invest in our account in terms of personnel, disinterested study of our problems and unstinting effort—and we know that we cannot get such investment except on the expectation of mutual building. Furthermore, we would not want effort deflected from the job in hand to the business of keeping us sold. To be very blunt, unless we are dissatisfied, unless because of new developments we need additional agencies, and unless we make our intention known to our agencies, we do not entertain bids for our business.

"As I have said, we treat our agencies as working partners and we put at their disposal all the information which we can. We expect in return that they shall be as concerned with the success of our efforts as we are. We expect in addition to all the creative and productive services of an agency the very best and most disinterested counsel, even to the point of advising us *not* to advertise if the facts so warrant. This frequently happens, believe it or not.

> (signed) Charles G. Mortimer, Jr.
> Vice President"

June 9

I said something the other day to the copy and art departments that I would like to say to everyone in the organization:

Foote, Cone & Belding is in business to make money.

But doing this successfully means a great deal more than the insurance of our jobs for three or four months, or a year. Most of all, it keeps our everlasting promise to our clients that their selling problems are our first concern.

The agency that once thinks first about itself is on its way to failure.

June 22

Some time ago I said in a talk to the Advertising Club that I believe a single exaggerated claim in a newspaper or magazine —or over the air—contaminates every other advertisement to which the reader or the listener is subjected—for days, or maybe weeks, or months.

Now, I would like to add that I think it also contaminates the person who writes it.

*(If this were not so, how could three different writers say
of three different analgesics that each works faster, lasts longer
and relieves headaches better than either of the others.*

*(There is a great argument here for saying that advertising
lies. Unfortunately, to refute the argument is impossible. One
can only hold that most advertisements, like most people, are
honest.*

*(Also, like most people, advertisements are prone to exag-
geration.)*

June 29

Any of us would be presumptuous to ever adapt the great
words of literature to ordinary advertising; but still—a cat can
look at a king, and I hope that none of you will pass by one of
the great books of our time, perhaps one of the greatest of
all time.

It is Winston Churchill's "The Gathering Storm," and I
would like to quote two front pages.

"MORAL OF THE WORK

In War: Resolution
In Defeat: Defiance
In Victory: Magnanimity
In Peace: Good will

"THEME OF THE VOLUME

How the English speaking peoples
through their unwisdom,
carelessness, and good nature
allowed the wicked
to rearm."

Rarely, I think have greater, simpler words been written.

July 9

There is a kind of popularity that I hope no one in this
company will ever earn.

This is the one that comes from answering questions or
simply talking about matters, however interesting, that have to
do with the affairs of our clients.

In a sense we are like lawyers and doctors and nurses, in
that our business is entirely other people's business. And we
must be no less vigilant in seeing to it that no detail of any of
this is ever divulged by us.

Incidentally, I discovered a long time ago that the way to learn a lot of secrets is by never telling any.

July 13

Charles Luckman's answer to Miss Bernice Fitz-Gibbon of Gimbel's re: advertising, at *Life's* Round Table, as reported in the current issue (July 12) makes some very good reading and some very good sense.

Having taken Miss Fitz-Gibbon fairly apart, Mr. Luckman made the major counterattack against the Round Table critics of advertising:

> " 'I must confess I have never been so confused and amazed in my life as at some of the statements made here. Advertising can only be a part of our economic system if it helps sell more and better products at lower cost. In order to sell more products you have to use advertising in a way that will sell products.' This means that advertising is closely bound to the cultural level of the people. For example, said Mr. Luckman, he himself once decided to take the soap operas off the air, on the grounds that their cultural level was too low. The result was that the company was deluged with protests and it had to put the soap operas back on again.

> "At this point Mr. Luckman turned the attack against his accusers. The trouble, he said, is not with the advertisers but with those whose task it is to enlighten the people and raise their cultural level: editors, educators and the clergy. The responsibility for the low cultural standards of the country lies with them, he declared. But instead of providing the necessary leadership, they too are merely meeting the demands of the people."

(Charles Luckman, onetime head of Pepsodent and later of Lever Brothers Company, now is one of the country's leading architects. Bernice Fitz-Gibbon was a widely acclaimed retail advertising executive.)

July 16

The silliest automobile advertising of all time is probably the series of magazine spreads for Chrysler which features wild horses, dogs, bears, ducks (in the latest)—everything but automobiles, over the signature 'the Beautiful Chrysler'.

At the other pole stands the nuts-and-bolts advertising of the new Ford.

Once more it is obvious that you can only have good advertising when you have *something to say* . . . and when you have, you'd better *say it straight*.

(Careful analysis will show that William Bernbach's twisting of an accepted proposition [Think Small] is a beautiful example of surprise in advertising. The reader is caught quite off guard.)

August 19

While one of the happiest things in the world of advertising and selling is a high-rating radio program, it is a very much more important economic fact that many a show with a modest rating helps make sales at ever so much less cost.

Audience turnover is one of the principal reasons.

Armour's afternoon "Hint Hunt", for example, has a summer Nielsen rating of around 4.0, a far cry from the wintertime "twenties" and "thirties" of the big nighttime programs. But in a six weeks period "Hint Hunt" is tuned in one or more times by more than 30% of all American homes . . .

Self-liquidating premiums and contests for small prizes regularly bring in from 100,000 to 250,000 labels, as proof of purchase, in a matter of two weeks!

August 24

Despite the satisfactory results of our several radio programs, I do not see how anyone in advertising can afford to be complacent about any radio program that cannot eventually lend itself to television.

Coincidental checks of homes which have both radio and television sets show the latter to be in use by as much as 15 to 1 over the former—even when radio's headliners are on the air.

Television isn't coming. It's here.

(Only Jack Benny and Bob Hope of 1948's top ten made the jump from radio to television. Fred Allen tried to beat back the new medium with ridicule and quickly lost out.)

September 7

Somehow or other I've always had the notion that Smith,

Jones and Brown are the commonest American names.

But the other day, waiting in a doctor's office, I picked up the new telephone directory and learned that in Chicago, at least, the Johnsons are way in the lead—with 62 columns of listings against 44 for the Smiths, 27 for the Browns and only 22 for the Jones . . .

There are eleven columns of names that begin with Sz (half as many as the Jones), seven that begin Cz (more than the Cooks or the Coopers). There is one whole column where each name starts with Czsz. There are ten different Stanley Szymanskis, ten Joseph Wozniaks (against ten Joseph Kennedys), four Helen Szymusiaks . . . three Joseph Szyszkas.

Altogether, the completely unillustrated telephone book presents a striking group picture of the many different peoples of Chicago—and America, to whom our advertising must appeal.

September 9

Any idea that somewhere in the current Nash motor car series there would surely come the worst poster of the year now is dispelled.

There is a new, dead sure cinch for the doubtful honor.

It shows a golfer who has just muffed a shot—looking ruefully at a caddy whose unconcerned whistling presumably has caused the shot to be dubbed.

The caption: *Next time get one that stays silent!*

The point (handled in a small panel at lower left): *Servel is the silent refrigerator*.

Something very bad has happened to a great deal of poster advertising. And I hope it never happens to ours.

Posters can still sell hard.

Or be *forceful* reminders.

They can't be merely cute.

October 19

One of the silliest food advertisements this writer has ever seen appeared two weeks ago in *Life* when National Biscuit Company took a blank page opposite a full color page for Ritz Crackers to say at the bottom in tiny 10 pt. type: "The Outstanding Cracker."

The spread cost $36,675.70 to show on the color page a Ritz package together with fourteen Ritz wafers and two rather ordinary looking pieces of cheese on a wooden server—over the words: "With cheese, nothing tastes as good as Ritz . . . but Ritz."

How much more this advertiser might have gotten for his money is illustrated by the Starch Report on a recent *Life* spread for Armour Pantry-Shelf Meals wherein 18% of *Life's* woman readers were indicated to have read most of the 575 words about six different Armour canned meats.

Food and food recipes are news, and a food advertiser who fails to take advantage of this fact blindly overlooks his greatest opportunity.

December 3

Foote, Cone & Belding continues in first place among advertising agencies for average evening radio program ratings according to the Nielsen Index for October. Our average is 11.6 . . .

We continue in seventh place in the daytime averages . . . Benton & Bowles is first; Dancer second; Compton and Young & Rubicam third; BBD&O fifth; Thompson sixth.

I think it should be noted that the ratings for the three front-running agencies in the daytime averages are largely the result of the excellent time periods acquired through the years by Procter & Gamble, General Mills and General Foods for their soap operas.

(The excellence of the time period results primarily from the juxtaposition of programs. It has little or nothing to do with the clock. With rare exceptions this holds as true for television as it did for radio. A strong preceding program is the prime factor in many a successful broadcast.)

1949

January 5

One of the easiest mistakes to make in the advertising business is for anyone writing or planning advertising to think that all people are very much like he or she is—that they like the same things and do the same things.

Almost every man I know plays golf. And talks about it practically continuously. If I were to go by my friends I would think golf scenes in advertising as for Hiram Walker or Dial

Soap or whatnot, would be very attractive. The facts, however, prove something else again.

A recent coast-to-coast study of men by Crossley, Inc. for *Argosy* magazine shows something less than 10% ever play golf.

Fishing, on the other hand, is engaged in, six or more times a year, by 39%.

(The number of men playing golf has undoubtedly increased greatly. But the sale of campers, trailers and boats indicates an increase also in fishing. It is easier than ever before to go where the fish are, and it wouldn't take much of an increase to maintain the ratio; particularly at the skyrocketing cost of golf.)

January 20

To me, *The New Yorker* has suddenly taken on a new significance and one to which no other magazine I know has ever aspired.

It has refused to run a perfectly decent, honest advertisement for one of our most respectable clients for the simple reason that, in *The New Yorker's* judgment, it simply wasn't — interesting!

The advertisement was one supplied to Marshall Field & Company by a sweater manufacturer. *The New Yorker* informed Field's that they had already run a similar page for the sweater people and that to show the same not-too-exciting sweater again would really be cheating their readers who are looking for *news* about clothes and where to get them.

When other publishers take an equal interest in making advertising work — and not just printing it — advertising will have taken a big step up.

January 26

Someone was talking, the other day, about the thrills in the advertising business. I argued that any business can be thrilling.

But it wasn't until I went to bed last night that I thought of a case to prove my point.

* *

Years ago, when I was a clerk in the classified department of the *San Francisco Examiner,* one of my jobs was to take in the death notices.

It was a dreary routine.

But it had one high spot.

It came late on a Sunday afternoon when a hatless man fairly flew into the office, planked down a typewritten form on the counter and literally shouted:

"We got him! We got him!"

The form told the story.

President Harding had died that morning, after a very short illness, in San Francisco's Palace Hotel. And the man who was flying three feet off the ground was the appointed undertaker.

He was the happiest man I have ever seen.

February 14

Some day I may have to eat this memo.

But I don't think I shall.

In a long interview in *The Tribune,* Mr. Spyro Skouras, Chairman of Twentieth Century-Fox, sees the great future of television bound up with the movies and movie houses. He envisions new films televised simultaneously to thousands of theatres across the country, eliminating prints and their transportation, and much of the theatre's mechanics.

I think Mr. Skouras is whistling as he approaches a graveyard.

For if there is one thing that television seems most likely to eliminate, it is the moving picture theatre.

It is possible already to be entertained in your own living room with a variety and quality of entertainment that on many nights tops anything most movie theatres now offer.

The variety is going to increase and the quality is going to get better.

And I would bet all the tea I have that the movies will compete only *inside* the American home.

Some way will be found to charge home viewers for supershows of all kinds. Perhaps the way lies in Zenith Radio's Phone-vision—whereby a scrambled television image is cleared through a telephone connection.

But whatever the way, entertainment at home—via television, promises to change the whole pattern of American life after dark.

That it will change advertising too, to a greater extent than even radio has, cannot be disputed.

(I refuse to give up on pay television. So far it has been stymied by the entrenched interests. But if there is ever going to be variety and quality in broadcasting, the viewer is going to have to share the cost.)

February 15

One of the most refreshing things that comes regularly in my mail is the Wedge, a tiny publication that is issued monthly by Batten, Barton, Durstine & Osborn.

In the latest issue there appears the following item:

"December 15, 1948—On the first of last July the subway fare in New York City went up to 10 cents.

"For almost six months now I've been delayed in front of the turnstiles by people, usually women, who are still trying to use nickels.

"I've cursed them silently, or chuckled sympathetically, depending on my mood. People are naturally hard to change once they get a habit.

"Today, I got stuck in the turnstile. It just wouldn't work. People lined up behind me, muttering, some not any too politely.

" 'Damn,' I thought. 'They've done something to these slots. I can't get a nickel into them.'

"And then I said, 'Excuse me,' and slunk off into a corner to see if, maybe, I couldn't find a dime in *my* change pocket.

"If it's this tough to change a simple habit, what a job an advertiser faces when he tries to switch customers to his brand. It's not a job that can be done overnight —or by an in-and-out schedule."

The Wedge is copyrighted. But I am sure BBD&O won't mind this infringement of a thought that is so important to *all* advertisers.

February 18

I have said this before, but perhaps it should be frequently repeated—that there is no advertisement so good as one that performs a service in itself.

Sometimes this is because it contains real news.

Other times it is because it is filled with useful information.

Again, it may *prove* an important promise.

And I hope that we will never make an advertisement—for print or for the air, that does not interestingly and compellingly offer one or another of these things directly to the reader or listener.

It isn't enough simply to say "buy this" or "do that." We must *convincingly* tell *why*.

(The advertising of polyester double-knit clothing is a contemporary example, as is most Sears, Roebuck advertising. But the world didn't have to wait all this long for news in advertising. The food people with their menus and their recipes have been putting it into print for seventy years. Now, in television, this has become more common than ever.)

April 22

It is just possible that the present sales depression in a number of lines reflects not only the average consumer's conviction that if he holds on to his money a little longer each dollar will buy a little more, but also this fact: total advertising is at a 30% lower ratio to the national income than it was in 1940.

A great deal of the selling pressure that was relaxed during the war has not been reapplied. And until it is, I think we have little reason to expect a sustained high level of sales.

May 10

The economics of good advertising, adequately financed (to gain both necessary circulation and proper penetration) rarely is better illustrated than in the 1948 annual report of the International Cellucotton Products Company.

Sales of both Kleenex and Kotex reached all-time highs.

The company's profit reached its all-time top.

Advertising expenditures were the greatest in the company's history.

But the ratio of advertising to sales and profits—the cost of advertising—was the lowest on the company's records.

Furthermore, had the Cellucotton company somehow achieved the same total of sales without spending a dollar for advertising, the savings to consumers could not have been passed on, for there is no coin small enough to represent the savings on a single package of either product.

This is something that even some economists (?) forget about the business we are in.

(The above could be dated 1972 and there would be no change except in the name of the advertiser. International Cellucotton Products Company, a marketing company, was absorbed by its parent Kimberly-Clark Corporation in 1952.

(This is not to say that advertising never adds to the selling price of anything. It is a large item in most luxury goods and non-necessities, but it adds little or nothing to the price consumers pay for most products of frequent purchase. Volume pays the advertising bill.)

May 16

I have just realized what it is that Americans do when they would rather not do anything—about something.

They form a committee.

A committee is a group of three or more men or women who manage to take from three weeks to three years to do what one person could do in half an hour of either concentration or good hard work.

A committee is a device to put off indefinitely the making of a decision.

It is a shield behind which to retreat, hoping that somehow the retreat will become an advance—with somebody else carrying the spear.

May 19

When we talk about advertising as a selling force, it is well to remember that advertising *alone* sells very few things.

To be sure, it can and does sell goods by mail and book club memberships ... and stomach pills.

But most of the things that are advertised are actually *sold* in stores and salesrooms. And all the advertising in the world can't sell them if they aren't on sale—if proper distribution has not put them where they can be found.

Along with adequate distribution there is the matter of display ...

Advertising can build confidence and preference.

But it takes merchandising to make the sale.

The goods you want to sell must not be out of sight or out-displayed, or preference goes quickly out of mind.

May 31

We are a wonderful people.

A United States Steel advertisement in last week's *Saturday Evening Post* boasts that "the beautiful, wide, straight, smooth roads you've been wishing for, are really on their way . . . taking form at the rate of $700 million worth of construction per year."

A good deal of this $700 million is undoubtedly going for straightening roads, so that huge trailer-trucks and ever-lighter passenger cars can go faster and faster—and kill more people.

Another chunk is for cutting down trees, the clumps that the curves now go around.

You can see men at work destroying the beauty of the landscape all over the Middle West and West—in the interest of the trucks, and speed.

In the East, on the other hand, millions are being spent to replace straight, fast, ugly roads with gently-curving parkways —to cut down speed. And still more millions are going to plant and move in trees and shrubs and flowers.

Some day the West and Middle West will do the very same thing.

But this we'll do with *another* $700 million *multiplied by the years it will take.*

(I seemed to have been interested in ecology before I had ever heard the word. How I managed to omit signs and billboards in the above, I don't know, for they are among the chief despoilers of the landscape. The conditions attending the allocation of government highway funds have had a salutary effect on the large poster companies, but the proliferation of local signs for motels, eating places, cocktail lounges, antique shops, fruit stands, etc., goes on unabated.)

June 1

I think we could all agree that every advertisement should be a promise.

If this is the case, let's see if we can't do the following things with each one:

1) Make it important
2) Make it clear
3) Make it dramatic
4) Make it sincere
5) Make it sing
   and
6) Keep it as short as we can.

*(After monkeying with this from time to time, I have final-
ly arrived at the following, which I shan't tamper with again.*

*(Advertising is the business, or the art, if you please, of
telling someone something that should be important to him. It
is a substitute for talking to someone.*

*(It is the primary requirement of advertising to be clear,
clear as to exactly what the proposition is.*

*(If it isn't clear, and clear at a glance or a whisper, very
few people will take the time or the effort to try to figure it out.*

*(The second essential of advertising is that what must be
clear must also be important. The proposition must have value.*

*(Third, the proposition [the promise] that is both clear and
important must also have a personal appeal. It should be beamed
at its logical prospects; no one else matters.*

*(Fourth, the distinction in good advertising expresses the
personality of the advertisers; for a promise is only as good as
its maker.*

*(Finally, a good advertisement demands action. It asks for
an order, or it exacts a mental pledge.*

*(Altogether these things define a desirable advertisement
as one that will command attention but never be offensive.*

(It will be reasonable, but never dull.

(It will be original, but never self-conscious.

(It will be imaginative, but never misleading.

*(And because of what it is and what it is not, a properly
prepared advertisement will always be convincing and it will
make people act.)*

June 8

Fear of depression fills the air.

And fear is contagious.

I don't know that there is very much any of us can do about
it. But we certainly can think about the times we live in and try
to understand them better . . .

The fact is, almost every American could earn the real
necessities of life in something less than half his current working time. The rest of his hours of labor are for "luxuries."

When any large number of us decide to do without some of
these, or to postpone our purchases, a certain number of dollars
ceases to circulate.

June 20

There is a wonderful essay in *The New Yorker,* by John Davenport, on the subject of Slurvian.

Mr. Davenport puts it down that he first heard Slurvian spoken fluently by a man whose closest friend was a chap named Hard (Howard).

"Hard was once in an automobile accident, his car, unfortunately, cliding with another, causing Hard's wife Dorthy, who was with him, to claps." . . .

If you will rilly listen you will prolly find out that more than a few Slurvian words have crep into your own vocabulary.

Personny, I'm going to be a good deal more careful.

Personally, that is.

(True Slurvian always saves a syllable.)

August 1

The extra check herein is to keep a promise that I made early in February, and that I have mentioned several times since.

This represents your equal share of one half of our savings from the first six months' budget for light and power, telephone and telegraph, office supplies, messenger service and unbillable items.

The total savings amounted to $10,985. One half of this is $5,492.50. Dividing this equally between the eligible people (401) gives us $13.70 apiece—less the deductions that, unfortunately, we can never escape.

August 2

This is to recommend to you, indeed to urge you to read, a most frightening book.

The name: "1984."

The author: George Orwell.

"1984" is at once a satirical novel and a novel of suspense, but it is like no other you have ever read, for it is neither a satire on other novels or of manners, nor is it a mystery thriller.

It is simply the story of one unbeliever in a police-state of the future.

The setting is London, and the state has three cardinal principles: WAR IS PEACE, FREEDOM IS SLAVERY, IGNORANCE IS STRENGTH.

That the author is able to demonstrate these with maddening logic gives the book its terrifying force.

Buy it. Or borrow it. Or, if you must, steal it.

(The United States comes closer and closer to underwriting the first of Orwell's propositions. The massive bombing in Viet Nam was ordered piously to promote peace. Freedom in China is almost pure slavery. Freedom from the ravages of the warlords has been replaced by slavery under the state. Ignorance of the world outside is part of the vise that grips the Russian people. Thus, this fiction of 1949 is all around us in real life in 1973.)

August 8

Every once in a while someone wonders if the food people wouldn't be better off to forget menus and recipes and make their advertising strictly competitive.

Today I have a new study of the women who buy *Woman's Day* magazine, by Elmo Roper, wherein the following are named as the most important features in the perfect magazine:

Recipes and menus	by 61.9%
Home decoration	45.1
Bringing up children	29.5
Needlework	26.0
Home repairs	24.6
Short stories	21.1
Fashion and beauty	19.9
World and national affairs	18.2
Patterns	17.1
Novelettes	4.9
Movie reviews	4.3

There were 2,006 respondents. And just to check on the above, they were asked which things, if any, they would choose to see given only a little space, or left out entirely in the ideal magazine. The answers form the exact reverse of the pattern above. Thirty per cent wanted nothing left out, 23.3% could do without the movie reviews. Only 1.1% without the recipes and menus.

September 12

Most of you know that I think the Community Fund performs a vital welfare function — sufficiently vital, in fact, to cause me to serve as a member of the Board of Directors and Chairman of the Campaign Planning Committee.

What you may not know is why I think it is important — why I believe that every person who earns wages has a definite obligation to support the Community Fund with his or her time and mind and money.

Sociologists tell us that welfare needs are bred out of the concentrations of population in industrial centers.

Concentrations of population are created by the demands of mass production industry for a labor market.

Our standard of living—our present jobs—this firm—would not exist except for the thing we call mass production.

From the start of the Industrial Revolution, society has paid for its higher living standards in loss of the individual laborer's adaptability. Out of concentrations of population, labor specialization and lowered adaptability stem welfare needs.

Recognizing the relationship between welfare needs and the existence of mass production industry, the Community Fund idea was developed by American business people as a voluntary means of bridging the gap between the income and outgo of neighborhood welfare agencies. They knew too that should the voluntary program fail, a bureaucratic substitute would be devised providing less benefit at greatly increased cost to us all.

(Chicago's Community Fund is the most successful in the country. The reason lies in a lesson learned long ago. Business firms are solicited at the top by teams of recognized business leaders. Individuals are solicited where they work by teams of their co-workers. All according to a formula based for industry and commerce on the number of employees in each place of business; for executives, one per cent of annual income; for workers, one day's pay.

(The Chicago Community Fund, unlike most others, has achieved its goal every year since 1961.)

September 28

BAR SOAP
probably Kills as many Women as Bar-rooms
do Men. Why isn't this Habit of Overwork at
the Washtub — the most Unwomanly, Unnatural, Unhealthy kind of Labor — why isn't
this Denounced like the Drink Habit?

The above, believe it or not, is the lead in an advertisement for Pyle's Pearline washing compound in *The Delineator,* for November, 1909.

I have always heard that this once successful soap powder went out of business because the proprietor stopped advertising. Now I think I know better.

October 19

Jim Cornell recently sent Hugh Davis some information that indicates what happens to radio listening in television homes.

Using Pulse (coincidental) ratings for New York, we find the picture almost unvarying:

	All Homes	TV Homes	
Walter Winchell	23.3	2.7	(12%)
Theatre Guild	13.5	1.9	(14%)
Louella Parsons	13.7	1.3	(9%)
Red Skelton	14.2	2.4	(17%)
Break the Bank	11.3	.3	(3%)
The Fat Man	13.5	1.7	(13%)
Milton Berle	14.2	1.7	(12%)
Godfrey's Talent Scouts	15.0	.7	(5%)
Inner Sanctum	13.5	1.3	(10%)
Lux Radio Theatre	23.2	3.7	(16%)
Average	15.5	1.8	(12%)

October 25

Perhaps it is inevitable that little boys who write and draw on newly painted fences and record their initials for posterity in the soft cement of fresh-laid sidewalks shall grow up into men who put signs on any and every available wall—often for less than no reason at all.

The temptation that exists in blank space is simply too strong for the average man. He has to fill that space, somehow, wherever he finds it. And if he can call the result of his efforts Advertising, he feels a warm, sweet glow.

One result of this temptation, which I noted last week riding West, is the violation of honest, if shabby freight car sides, where soiled, blurred letters on a hump-backed boxcar proclaim the Delaware & Lackawanna *the Route of Phoebe Snow,* where the Chesapeake & Ohio's promise to be *the Progressive Railroad*

is written on a rusty gondola . . . and even the Santa Fe calls
attention to its *extra-fast, extra-fine, extra-fare Super-Chief* on
the soot-streaked yellow sides of some of its most dilapidated
old reefers.

Technically, I suppose this is advertising. But I can't believe that it is very good advertising.

To be sure it is cheap.

But, like the dirty wallsigns, harassed and faded by the
elements, it is also cheapening—to the very things it seeks to
glorify.

November 7

Sheer cleverness in advertising rarely is good business. Ex-
tra-smart most often means outsmart, and the victim is usually
the advertiser himself.

A recent Heinz four-color bleed spread in the *Ladies' Home
Journal* is a beautiful example.

Alongside the principal illustration of baked beans in a
crock (with a couple of Heinz tins dim in the background) is a
panel entitled "OLD BEAN RECIPE". Then, following this
admonition, "If you insist upon baking your own beans, and we
wish you wouldn't, here's a grand old recipe"—there are the full
list of ingredients and all details.

The result of this cleverness, according to the Starch rating
figures, is that almost twice as many women (19%) read the
homemade recipe as read how Heinz makes good beans, too
(10%).

All this in $38,000 worth of space.

November 16

Both the Chicago and New York offices this week are guilty
of some needless (and quite unbelievable) superlatives.

Our own, in an advertisement in *Life,* blithely calls Chiffon
"America's finest soap flakes." The other, also in *Life,* talks
about "the smartest home-happiness idea in years," and adds,
"that's what thousands are saying about the new Emersons."

The important *fact* about Chiffon is that it is pure soap; it
has no filler like the granulated type that most people use.

However, I cannot believe that other PURE soap — like
Ivory Flakes, for instance, is not equally fine. And I do not believe that anyone, anywhere (let alone thousands) would ever

call any radio set—or anything else, the smartest home-happiness idea in years.

Advertising license may be all right with the Federal Trade Commission, which calls the kind above, legitimate trade puffery; but I think *we* should be above it. I think that every one of us should shun advertisingese like the plague — for (like the plague) it is highly contagious, and dangerous to *all* advertising.

December 1

Advertising for men's apparel continues to be something more than just a challenge to advertising people; more often than not it beats them in straight falls.

After a long and gallant stand, Young & Rubicam and Cluett, Peabody finally have been pinned to the mat by a series of advertisements for Arrow Shirts as loony as anything Manhattan or Van Heusen ever have done to help make men's wear copy the battiest stuff in print.

At the moment, only BBD&O and Hart, Schaffner & Marx still are on their feet in a lunatic business whose latest offense is a color page in the *Chicago Sunday Tribune,* under the headline:

Pale-face feet now dance for joy!

Esquire Colorfixt Socks in 17 Indian Warrior Colors—

Won't run! Won't fade!

Beneath this gem a painted brave, complete with tomahawk, offers a choice of the seventeen bilious shades for "peewee wampum—75 cents . . . at your men's wear *tepee.*"

Ugh.

1950

March 15

Julian Watkins has put together an enormously interesting collection entitled, "The 100 Greatest Advertisements" that I have sent to the library.

It is easy to agree with most of the selections. But here and there one runs across a campaign that for all its bright appearance must be written down as a failure. Such a one is the "Modess . . . because" campaign that Mr. Watkins has singled out.

The fact is, Kotex has been running away from Modess faster in the months since this campaign began than at any other time during the past seven years. Currently Kotex has almost 73% of the total market and its rate of increase was fastest during the last four months of 1949—which was after the chosen Modess campaign had been running about a year.

(Johnson & Johnson must have known something about this Modess advertising that I couldn't discover, for after publishing various alternatives they returned to it time and again, with the original format and lack of any supporting text.)

May 16

I have had something to say from time to time about dishonest advertising and advertising that is in bad taste . . . and also about advertising license.

The latter is the thing that is dignified by the Federal Trade Commission as "legitimate trade puffery." And I think it is as bad as either of the others.

We should have no part of any of them.

Nor with silly superlatives.

On successive pages of the *New York Times* for last Friday I saw the same twelve and one-half inch television screen called a *big* 12½, a *huge* 12½ and a *giant* 12½!

So help me.

May 25

Foote, Cone & Belding has agreed to handle the magazine and newspaper advertising for United States Savings Bonds for the Treasury Department.

This is the world's largest advertising campaign.

The advertisements appear monthly in full page space in 1,950 magazines. Weekly advertisements are furnished newspapers in both full page and 400-line size.

The space is donated to the government, on regular schedule, and there is no commission.

The advertising will be produced by the Chicago office, under the direction of The Advertising Council.

June 6

Foote, Cone & Belding continues to operate in an almost fantastic confusion of names.

Recently we received a parcel addressed to Mr. Foote, Librarian, c/o Fairfax, Cone & Belding.

Last week I had a letter (asking for a donation, too) sent in care of Toote Cone & Beeding.

And now Vincent Tutching sends one from Montreal addressed to Foote, Conan & Doyle.

October 18

It is impossible to return from even a few days' trip to Southern California without feeling that people in the Middle West and in the East are missing a good deal of good living simply through the force of old habits.

It is easy to laugh at the sheer exuberance of Southern California—where dog food is sold at a Pet Pantry and the good honest hamburger masquerades as ground roundburger, beefburger, primeburger, sirloinburger, basketburger, mushroomburger . . . and, believe it or not, just plain burger—charcoal grilled!

One may smile a little at Beauty Bazaars and Kookie Kubberds and slendo-therapy and 5 minute soft-water car washing. But the cars are clean and shiny and the girls are slim . . .

With a metropolitan population roughly the size of Chicago's, one sees scores of huge shopping centers clustered around great department stores and spanking specialty shops and super super-markets—each with acres of free parking space.

And if double-header diesel trucks rumble at fifty and sixty miles an hour, they do it on four-lane newly paved highways broadly divided at the center; and private car freeways to Hollywood, Santa Ana and the Harbor soon will join with the Pasadena freeway to criss-cross Los Angeles without a stop-light or a crossing—where only a little while ago Chicago-loop congestion reigned . . .

Factories are everywhere.

And spread around them, new subdivisions—not with the backyard swimming pools that abound in Beverly Hills, but with gardens setting off even the smallest clean-painted houses, giving them light and air . . .

But I think the most amazing—and perhaps, the most significant thing about Southern California is the almost complete oblivion of the people there, to distance. They have not been afraid to spread out. And they have done this to make a kind of

free and gracious living that is in a hundred ways unique . . .
Southern California is an astonishing place.

October 23

Mr. Dieter has sent me the following from Bob Foreman's
column "Listening and Looking" in *Advertising Agency:*

"Robert Louis Stevenson said that literary art is
achieved by writers who know what to leave out. The
same might well be said in preparation of commercial
films for television. Not art—but selling impact . . .
memory value. This was proved most dramatically to
me in two one-minute spot-films for Bromo-Seltzer on
which I recently worked. The first was a slickly produced, cast and directed job of a commuter on a railroad station platform who suffers a headache. The
train comes in—but it's the Bromo-Seltzer train which
speeds his relief, etc. There was live action, animation
and a large mock-up of the Bromo-Seltzer train in
which the live actor rode away. On paper the thing
seemed to play. One of the top film producers did the
job and did it well. But . . .

"In contrast with Film No. 2, which consisted of Norman Brokenshire talking quietly, sincerely and convincingly about the product, it will not be anywhere
nearly so effective. There's too much in it. Too many
distractions. Too busy. There are TOO MANY things
to remember. The Brokenshire spot has two elements—
the man and the product. Each supplements the other.
There's a lesson in this which I for one am keeping in
mind for the three hundred spots that lie in the immediate future."

It seems to me that one of the great difficulties with television commercials is the attitude with which we too often approach their making.

It is as if we said, "Now we are going to make a television
production, what can we borrow from radio, what can we borrow from movie techniques, etc." . . . when what we really
should say to ourselves is this: "How can we *tell* somebody
something and how can we *show* somebody something in the
simplest possible way—to convince them why it is in *their own
best interest* to buy it and use it."

This has always been the job of advertising. And it has no other, in product promotion.

Radio gave us jingles and gimmicks of one kind and another only to try to make an impression on "tuned-out" ears.

Television plays to wide open ears—and eyes.

October 31

Talking the other night at the Creative Advertising Clinic of the C.F.A.C., Mr. Koretz had the following to say about words:

"Don't get into the habit of using the same tired old words that you see day in and day out—in ads in every magazine and newspaper—the ads people rarely bother to read. Even if it is hard to find *fresh* words—it's worth working at . . . and that's your job.

"Take this sentence, for instance—see if you think it has a fresh slant:

" 'The yellow leaves, like golden
saucers, lay in the shallow pool.'

"Or this one:

" 'The owls talked softly among
themselves for they liked the night.'

"And this:

" 'The last ember was extinguished as the
cold wind spoke down the chimney.'

"Those three sentences were written by 7th graders in a Highland Park grammar school *this year*. And they leave a lesson for all copywriters—for you and for me. We, too, can find fresh words. We can find fresh words —fresh headlines—fresh layouts—fresh ideas—if we try. If we constantly strive for new combinations. If we take the trouble to be discontented. If we fix our star on a desire to excel. If we work our ads—each and every part of them—over and over and over again."

November 27

The difference between most advertising people and people-in-advertising has probably never been better illustrated than by the violent reaction of the former to the opening guns in the Television Manufacturers' campaign to sell black and white receivers *now* in the face of the FCC approval of CBS color.

A fair sample of the appeal appears under the first newspaper headline, "There are some things a son or daughter *won't* tell you."

"How can a little girl describe a deep bruise inside? *No, your daughter won't ever tell you the humiliation she's felt in begging those precious hours of television from a neighbor.*"

This printed advertisement goes on and on in the same shoddy way, and the radio commercials are no less flagrant in playing cynically on deep human emotions.

The thing is, the furor over the campaign has been raised almost entirely by agency people and the advertising trade press. I have had a number of notes from our people. The 4A's has been deluged with protests. And every trade paper is filled with the chorus of disapproval.

To be sure, *an* advertising agency (Ruthrauff & Ryan) *did* prepare the campaign. But I know that we would have done no such thing; and I know hundreds of other agencies that wouldn't have either.

On the other hand there is no record of a newspaper turning the advertisements down or a radio station refusing to play the equally nauseous announcements. And the campaign is paid for by the following television manufacturers: RCA, General Electric, Westinghouse, Philco, Admiral, Motorola, Zenith, Emerson, Du Pont, Magnavox, Capehart, Stromberg-Carlson, Scott, Belmont, Sentinel, Sylvania, Pilot, Hoffman, Fada and Hallicrafters.

Together these people who have the most to gain from advertising have done it a disservice that no change now can modify—for they have used it shabbily and without conscience.

(The television manufacturers were years ahead of themselves in worrying about color television and, of course, the CBS system never got off the ground. As for the foolish advertising campaign, it mercifully expired after the initial reaction by the advertising industry.

(This was remarkable because, as far as I know, it remains the only campaign in history that was actually hooted out of print and off the air by advertising people themselves.

(One can only wish they would take on the television advertisers of men's exotic colognes and hair preparations.)

1951

January 19

For several years I have sent a brief personal report to our Chicago clients summing up our operations for the twelve months.

Today I am sending you a copy of the 1950 report exactly as it will be sent to our clients next week. [Much of the report was routine. Excerpts from it follow—Ed.]

I

The agency's total volume was $61,115,211. The 1949 volume was $51,416,005.

In Chicago the total was $27,970,647. In 1949 it was $27,-066,628.

A sharp increase in New York was accelerated by the transfer of the Pepsodent account to that office when its headquarters were moved from Chicago.

The Pacific Coast offices for the first time reached a total volume in excess of $10 million . . .

VI

Television continues to be the most exciting (and frequently the most exasperating) new thing in advertising.

Results are astonishing. On the other hand the freeze of facilities and the resulting scramble for available time in many cities, together with the complexity of delayed broadcasts (on film)—to say nothing of the problem of programming and costs, have made this the most difficult of all mediums for advertiser and agency alike.

Nevertheless, results are such that with no more than 10 million receiving sets in operation, desirable nighttime periods are completely sold out on the networks and free daytime periods are fast being taken up . . .

VIII

The most important change in Foote, Cone & Belding in 1950 was the resignation of Emerson Foote who, after a long illness and leave of absence, retired from the firm in October.

Mr. Foote's contributions to the first seven years of our operations were many and he will long be missed.

Mr. Belding has taken his place in New York.

IX

Our vision into the future is cloudy and uncertain.

We can only have faith that if we do our part along with every other business to help maintain America according to American standards—come what may, then we shall be successful together.

(The above was written when the affair in Korea was developing into a full-scale war. The government had seized the railroads to prevent a general strike. An attempt had been made to assassinate President Truman. The public was moody and restless.)

March 8

Speaking of selling, it is said that there are only eight reasons why a woman buys anything:

1) The husband says she can't have it.
2) It makes her look thin.
3) It comes from Paris.
4) The neighbors can't afford it.
5) Nobody's got one.
6) Everybody has one.
7) It's different.
8) Because.

If anyone knows why *men* buy things I'll be glad to pass the word along.

March 13

Someone said something to me the other day about our *resignation* of the Marshall Field & Company account and I would like to make a point about this.

We didn't resign the Marshall Field account. We were fired. And I hope that nobody will feel any need to try to hide the fact.

Field's own advertising department serves that huge business much as an advertising agency serves its clients—and with most of the facilities. One result, in our case, was that we were unable to maintain a satisfactory additional service on what amounted to a job basis.

It seems that an agency (this one, at least) can only do its best work when the work is of continuing importance. And this simply wasn't the case with our work for Field's.

I don't think this makes either of us either bad or boobs.

(The firing and hiring of advertising agencies usually occurs as a result of changes in the advertiser organization. New marketing executives and new advertising directors often want agencies of their own choosing, and get them. On the other hand, close association between principals generally produces long-lasting advertiser assignments.)

April 3

In *Time* (April 2) there appears an advertisement for Guckenheimer blended whiskey under the headline *America's Favorite*.

Since it is extremely doubtful if Guckenheimer is among the twenty top-selling brands, I couldn't help wondering how either the Alcohol Tax Unit of the U. S. Treasury Department (which must approve all distilled beverage advertising) or *Time* itself passed it.

And then I read the advertiser's signature. It was The American Distilling Company.

Good old Guckenheimer is (The) American (Distilling Company)'s Favorite—and my nomination for the most misleading headline of the year.

April 19

The advertising business still has a little way to go in the matter of morals.

Currently — newspapers, radio stations and outdoor plants across the country accord Hadacol the same welcome that they do fine, ethical products;

An appliance manufacturer whose washer is in second place in sales advertises it as America's favorite;

Kaiser automobile advertising features the "Fashion Academy Award" just as though this had been received in official industrywide competition instead of by arrangement;

And a pretty model used in a Toni ad for her naturally curly hair—which is compared to another pretty model's Toni wave—shows up in a rival home permanent advertisement as an implied user of that brand.

＊

Probably no one involved means any harm. But I think that honest advertising rates a better break.

May 4

I have a gripe against science.

It is about eggs and bananas and meat and melons.

It is about eggs that are all the same huge size and all the same color—inside as well as out, beautiful to look at but utterly without taste or character. It is about bananas that are uniformly ten inches long, uniformly yellow and unspoiled, and taste like soft plaster of paris. It is about the meat the butcher never hangs up to age for more than an hour. It is about melons that taste like squash.

And I wonder if just once more, I couldn't get a dozen eggs of something less than ostrich size; maybe with one brown one and one speckled one—and one with a little piece of feather stuck to the shell, from some chickens that root around in a barnyard and once in a while eat a worm.

I wonder if I couldn't have a single banana only six inches long—or four, streaked with black and maybe soft at one end, that smells sweet and tastes like a—banana.

I wonder if I couldn't have just one steak from a steer that *wasn't* Kansas City fed, that was ticketed to Boston or New York, and hung at the butcher's for two weeks. And I wonder if this summer I couldn't have one Cranshaw melon that hasn't been crossed with a gourd to make it ship better.

Science is a wonderful thing. But I'm sick of horsemeat and soya and gourds processed into eggs and meat and melons.

I want to enjoy what I eat, once more. I want to remember the way things used to taste—before they were perfected.

May 22

This seems to be open season on advertising and advertising people.

Close on the heels of Bernard DeVoto's diatribe in *Fortune*, Mr. Henry Seidel Canby in the June *Atlantic* illustrates a discussion of defeatist novels wherein the emphasis is on toughness and "every one looks his worst" with a reference to Fred Wakeman's *The Hucksters* and goes on to say that "there have been dozens (of novels) since . . . that, like the advertisements and promotion that is the business of so many of their characters, are expertly and sometimes brilliantly written."

The only assumption one can draw (assuming that there *have* been dozens of such novels since, which I very seriously doubt) is that expertly and sometimes brilliantly written advertisements and promotion are something very bad indeed. And I wonder if Mr. Canby's ideas may not be too largely drawn from contemplation of the bosomy advertising and provocative promotion of the Book-of-the-Month Club—of which he is chairman of the Board of Judges?

Actually, I suppose there is no other kind of advertising that is so shallow (no matter how expertly it may be written) and so dishonest as book advertising, where fully half the quotes of approval from reviews that I have read are taken out of context.

May 24

Victor Ratner, advertising and promotion chief of Macy's, told me the other day that there are no crises in Macy's advertising department.

With 100,000 customers on a slow day, 350,000 on a busy one, the wheels simply have to keep turning. And with 60 to 70 full-page newspaper ads to be got out each week, one ad held up would gum the whole production.

The result: the ads go through the way they are planned—without change. Since they help to move $100 million worth of goods a year, I wonder if we may not worry and stew unduly about each word and phrase and every little layout detail in almost everything that goes through Foote, Cone & Belding.

Perhaps if we would just be as direct as we know how, and cut down on tricks (in broadcasting as well as in print), we could live more peacefully too.

June 5

Ernie Eversz the other day referred to the current Ethyl Gasoline magazine campaign ("There's a big difference between a perch and a percheron") as one of the silliest series of recent memory. And I agree with him; its over-reaching is so ridiculous as to make it stand out.

The Maidenform Bra campaign is another of the same kind ("I dreamed I went shopping in my Maidenform bra") and while I am sure that both of these would have a high recall score, I trust that we will never be tempted by any such hocus-pocus.

Advertising that is remembered *as advertising* rather than as a piece of news or good advice is rarely advertising at all.

*(The difference here is between advertising and paid pub-
licity, and Maidenform did very well with the latter until Playtex entered the field [which they now dominate] with reason-
why advertising.)*

June 14

The time spent watching America's 11 million television
sets is not new time. It has to come from somewhere.

Evenings, for instance. It has to come either from time
formerly spent movie-going, card-playing, visiting, reading,
sleeping or just dawdling. And I think it is a safe bet that
movies and reading are suffering most (radio listening, of
course, is off, but the radio shares its hours; children study by
it, adults play cards or read during broadcasts, etc.).

If I am right about reading, then book reading, magazine
reading and newspaper reading should give way to television
viewing in approximately this order because this is the order of
their popularity.

The thing that should concern us (in business) is the de-
creasing time spent with magazines and newspapers. Since
neither general magazine nor newspaper circulation is actually
dropping, I think we must conclude that it is individual articles
and stories and advertisements that must give up the time first.

And our job will be to make *our* advertisements important
enough, strong enough, clear enough and brief enough to work
against an entirely new urge—to turn the page and get on.

I don't think that magazines and newspapers will ever die.
But I do think that a lot of printed advertising will be worthless
unless its pace is changed.

We have always competed for interest within the pages of
our newspapers and periodicals. Now there is a huge and growing outside interest, too — competing with all printed matter
for *time.*

*(I couldn't have been more wrong about book reading. It
has grown by leaps and bounds since the above was written, and
I don't know why. The twenty-five cent paperbacks may have
had something to do with the initial spurt. But now the paperbacks range upward from a dollar to three dollars and a half,
and sales keep mounting.*

*(Incidentally, this is a phenomenon that advertising appar-
ently has had little or nothing to do with. Publishers tell me*

*that no book that won't sell without advertising will sell with it,
however much advertising is used.)*

July 9

This is written in London at Claridge's Hotel on Monday
afternoon, July 9 . . .

*

London is spick and span, clean and brightly polished, and
except around St. Paul's and the railway stations and the docks
along the Thames there are only occasional signs of the havoc of
the Blitz.

I had been told that London would be shabby and its people
shabbier, but we haven't seen this.

Living *is* austere. There is very little meat and very little
butter or other fat, few eggs; and clothing—between high prices
and limiting ration coupons—is very hard to come by.

But London has character and so, obviously, have its people. And in a quiet way I think it is rather gay. Maybe it is the
narrow, curving streets and the thousands of small shops and
the multi-colored store fronts and the tiny taxis that give it the
air of a vast and slightly Lilliputian bazaar beside the huge
public buildings.

But I think it is more than this. I think it has something to
do with that phrase: There will always be an England. And besides, this is Festival year!

August 16

Most people in advertising are aware of the huge waste that
is involved when display material grows old and wrinkled in retailers' stockrooms instead of in the windows and on the coun-
ters for which it was made—and paid for.

What I don't think most people in advertising realize is that
even when it is installed, many a window display is worth just
about nothing. This is particularly true in drug stores.

Checking the other day in New York, in mid-town Manhattan, I discovered that something more than half of the considerable number of Toni windows were rendered worthless by the
welter of the drug stores' own signs pasted on the glass in
front of the displays.

In a number of cases, in addition to the druggists' announcements of specials—on everything from hamburgers to

nylons to garden hose, there were more than a few manufacturers' posters helping to hide the displays.

The thing to remember is that you may have a great many units reported in use that *are* in use, yet almost entirely without effect.

Window and counter displays should be subjected to something a little more penetrating than quantitative reporting and checking.

August 27

Once upon a time there was an Advertising Agent who had a brand new Client and he got a Great Idea.

He would illustrate this Client's copy with the work of a big, important Illustrator who had never Stooped to do Commercial Stuff.

And so the Advertising Agent went to see the big, important Illustrator and he talked to him. And he sold him the Idea.

After a while the first Picture came.

And there was a Kind of Odor about it.

In fact, it Stunk.

Now, fortunately for the Advertising Agent, the Company had a couple of Art Directors who had some Sense. And whilst the Agent was making his Deal with the big, important Illustrator, and waiting for the Result, the Art Directors were having some Photographs made by a Professional Photographer who Loved to do Commercial Work.

And These were very, very Good.

So Everything came out All Right.

Except that the Company now owns one completely unusable Hand Painting that someone can have for his Cellar for Two Cents on the Dollar.

*

I wish this was only a Fable.

Actually, the Foolish Agent was named F. M. Cone. The new Client was Libby. And the Sensible Art Directors were Mr. D. Lockwood and Mr. F. Johnson—who up to this minute have not Mentioned the Incident; at least, loud enough for the Foolish Agent to hear.

August 29

The seven months' statement of Foote, Cone & Belding

shows a very important change in the breakdown of our volume when compared with 1950.

Last year radio (which was down from 1949) accounted for 17%, television for a little less than 3.

This year radio accounts for 19% and *television for* a leaping *11%*.

Outdoor and transportation remains even at 11%. And newspapers and magazines are down from 69 to 59%.

All this on an over-all 20% expansion in our volume.

(In 1972 television amounted to 59% of the agency's billing. Magazines accounted for 29%. Newspapers 9%. Radio 3%.)

August 31

Mr. Joseph P. Spang, Jr., president of the Gillette Safety Razor Company, has sent me a beautifully printed copy of a delightfully humorous and largely inspiring talk which he made recently before the members of the Newcomen Society in Boston on the occasion of Gillette's 50th anniversary.

A whole section has to do with beards which I, for one, learned about for the very first time:

"Beards have been, depending upon the swing of history, a conclusive sign of manliness; a mark of dignity; a mortal danger to warriors; a stamp of uncouthness—even insanity. The clean-shaven face at other times through the centuries have signified extreme youth or effeminacy, or identified a man's occupation, or signalled his degree of civilization. . . .

"Alexander the Great, realistic commander that he was, considered the beard a downright menace to his Macedonian troops. . . .

"With the collapse of Roman civilization and the surge of barbarous peoples throughout Europe, the beard became a symbol of full-grown manhood; only boys and eunuchs went without one. Consequently, to be shaved was a terrible humiliation. . . .

"In Europe, until thirty or forty years ago, to be smooth shaven was an indication that a man was an actor, a servant, or a priest. Footmen whose attire was the court dress—knee breeches and white silk stockings—had to be clean shaven. Also butlers, coachmen, grooms, jockeys, and hunt whips had to be clean shaven. But the chauffeur, a newer type of servant with no tradition back of him, was allowed to be mustached.

*

"Up to the advent of the safety razor, men had resented any rule that tampered with their beards or whiskers. As an example, in 1907, there was a serious waiters' strike in Paris against the rule of hotels that waiters must be clean shaven.

*

"Thus it can be readily seen that man's beard has played its role in our changing history. And though the problem of man's beard, and what to do with it, dates back thousands of years, it was not until 50 years ago that a slow, painful, even dangerous operation— shaving — was changed to one which could be performed with speed, ease, and comfort."

(Despite the beards that grow all around us, there are presently on the market, and heavily advertised, six electric shavers and at least as many razor blades, single and double; and blade sales increase 5% annually.

(The American male is a difficult animal to teach new tricks. Unlike his wife or her girlfriends, he likes to be the last to try new things.)

September 27

Great advertising campaigns are the result of good copy "thinking" rather than tricks with words.

The *service advertising* of Kotex (Are You in the Know), the Miss Rheingold *annual contest,* the Playtex Girdle *demonstrations* (by means of stroboscopic photographs), the Toni *demonstrations* (Which Twin has the Toni), the Sunkist *promise* (Sunkist lemonade in just six seconds) and Frigidaire's *answer to a problem* (the refrigerator made for once-a-week shopping)—all are examples of this fact.

What I think we should all strive for is a continuous effort to replace these—and every other campaign that we now are running, with something even better; something with still greater impact, something even more penetrating.

Maybe we can't do this.

But trying will be very good for our souls.
And very bad for complacency.

October 11

When the book *100,000,000 Guinea Pigs* was published, it created something of a sensation in what we might call the upper-middle intellectual circles. Now there is another book called *The Mechanical Bride* by Professor Herbert Marshall McLuhan which on the dust cover is called a psychological *100,000,000 Guinea Pigs* for "it reveals the insidious emotional appeals used by present-day advertisers, columnists, creators of comic strips, etc."

Most of the pages of the book deal with advertising, and they take apart individual advertisements and campaigns unmercifully. With most of the specific criticism it is easy to agree, but the implications that all advertising is bad is patently absurd.

Professor McLuhan feels that mass production has done little or nothing for American civilization and his analysis of what he calls "the familiar men of distinction, the feminine legs on a pedestal, the caressing prose describing the sleek body of a car, the everlasting promises to guarantee everlasting youth" is biting and sarcastic and lively.

McLuhan longs for the good old days. And one wonders if he really knows much about them.

I wonder, for instance, if he has ever looked at the advertising that was appearing at the turn of the century. This piece of copy (which Ford Sibley found in an old copy of the *Saturday Evening Post*) is fairly typical of 1906 production:

"THE JOYS OF LIVING

"NABISCO—sweet finale to the symphony of dining. Dessert confections most delicious and suggestive, Nabiscos melt in the mouth like the fairy food of fancy, and in melting yield a bewitching flavor. With Nabisco, conversation rallies, wit flashes and romance sheds enchantment over all. Then, serene and in harmony with themselves and all mankind,

your guests begin to appreciate the
true joys of living.
NATIONAL BISCUIT COMPANY"

October 17

One of the least inspiring things in advertising is a solid
block of copy—even under an intriguing headline.

Not always can one break up copy into captions beneath
pictures, or balloons as in the current Birds Eye advertisements
in magazines.

But we can break up the solid blocks.

We can write *short* paragraphs.

We can use *subheads*.

Or we can start some paragraphs (and particularly the
lead ones) with *bold initials*.

And we can run certain paragraphs (or even sentences) in
italics or bold face types.

The thing is: we should plan and write our advertisements
with all the possibilities of paragraphing and type arrangement
firmly in mind.

Otherwise many, many people will fail to read our words.

(Incidentally, for years I personally typed every ad I wrote
to measure; to make sure that a paragraph never ended at a
column end—where any reader I had got could so easily stop.)

October 23

We have just completed what may be the largest newspaper schedule in advertising history, in terms of the number
of individual advertisements and the brief period of time in
which they are to appear.

The number of the advertisements is 560, and they will appear within the space of four weeks for the Community Fund
of Chicago. Beginning last Monday ten of the ads appeared each
day—through Friday, in each of the four Chicago papers; and
each was different.

This week there are eight ads in each paper, each day; next
week there will be six, and in the fourth week, four; 1 column x 4
inch testimonials from real people (who are photographed) and
who will tell why *they* are contributing to the Fund in 1951.

The campaign, which is the Fund's first use of paid advertising, has been the subject of a great deal of comment . . . all good.

And the Fund officials are delighted.

November 8

In a brilliant talk before the 4A's at Coronado, in California, two weeks ago, Earle Ludgin explored an idea that has significance for everyone in advertising.

Borrowing a little from the engineers and their knowledge of the fatigue of metals, Mr. Ludgin said that the public mind and the public ear may in their own way be made to suffer from the *fatigue of believability* — brought on by advertising that even if not actually false or distorted, nevertheless is continuously and incessantly extravagant.

Mr. Ludgin went on to suggest that we look at the advertising we make with one question always in our minds:

Is it believable?

If it isn't, if we add in any way to the *fatigue of believability,* then we do both ourselves and our medium the greatest possible disservice.

And in the long run we do our clients the greatest disservice of all.

(There is a great deal of difference between truth and believability. I live with a woman who constantly challenges the truth of television commercials that I am sure have been checked out in laboratories and field tests for absolute accuracy. The trouble is, absurd slice-of-life scenes and far-fetched demonstrations are often contrary to the viewers' own experience and so rejected as untrue.

(Outrageous people like Folger's Mrs. Olsen, who carries a can of coffee in her bag wherever she goes, can be [and are] accepted as purely imaginary. But instantly cleaned and polished linoleum without so much as leaning on the mop, for example, is so incredible as to be labeled by any experienced housekeeper a sheer exaggeration.)

November 13

When I heard Arthur Godfrey say in a recent television commercial that a panel of professors at the University of New Hampshire had reviewed all cigaret advertising and found that only Chesterfield tells the truth, I could hardly believe my ears.

Now I am even more at a loss to understand either Godfrey, Liggett & Myers or the agency involved.

For the Better Business Bureau has bulletined its members to the effect that the panel was *not* a University of New Hampshire panel but a strictly private enterprise; that even so, it did *not* examine all cigaret advertising; that it did *not* say that only Chesterfield tells the truth; and, finally that the Chesterfield advertising it did review was *not* the campaign that Godfrey so piously pointed to.

This is the campaign that promises *no cigaret after-taste.*

And so Chesterfield has added to the stupid business of tearing down *other* advertising, the stupidest business of all: plain dishonesty.

November 15

Not to be outdone by Chesterfield, Lucky Strike now has embarked on a campaign of advertising that adds to Earle Ludgin's "fatigue of believability" as surely as if it had had no other aim.

Lucky Strikes, we are told—on television and radio and in the press—are *better made* than any other cigarets, and there are bar charts and sworn statements to prove it.

The only trouble is, we are *not* told what better made means. And the sworn statements only swear that the charts have been examined and are correct.

If it is doubtful that any such dubious campaign can help Luckies' ailing sales, its effect on advertising itself will likely be sharp and swift: another ugly black eye on the face of credibility.

November 16

One of the most interesting things about the current Lucky Strike campaign in newspapers is the use of the Hitler Big Lie technique applied to layout.

Having nothing whatever to say that is either pointed or appealing, Lucky Strike says it in 96 point type, hoping just by the size of the type, I gather, to make the mealy words seem important.

George W. Hill used large type, too, on occasion. But he

used it to put over *ideas*. When he wanted to say "better made" he said *so round, so firm, so fully packed—so free and easy on the draw,* and you knew what he was talking about.

He also talked about fine tobacco in cigarets and *proved* that Luckies bought just that.

The present campaign would seem to have been made by someone in full flight—and awful fright.

It is scared advertising.

And good advertising is always confident, and honest in appearance as well as appeal.

December 6

If anyone ever wants to know why I find the advertising agency business so fascinating I will tell him about my last week.

On Monday I attended a Frigidaire meeting at General Motors in Detroit. On Tuesday, a meeting of The Advertising Council. On Wednesday (in New York), a session with Van Raalte. On Thursday, Hallmark. On Friday, General Foods. On Saturday (back in Chicago), Armour soap. And on Sunday, I wrote copy all day for Hiram Walker.

Thus, in seven days I was concerned with whiskey, soap, cereals, greeting cards, hosiery, underwear and gloves, the Armed Forces blood bank, the steel scrap drive, and electric appliances . . . and with magazine, newspaper, outdoor, radio and television plans and copy.

In some businesses I suppose this would seem hugely mixed up.

But here there is a common denominator: *people.*

In a large sense, it is people that are our business. Finding out some of their wants and why, and how and where and when they buy, and what they will do under this or that urging, is the most fun I can think of.

December 17

There are very few better people in advertising than Victor Ratner, Vice President of Macy's, in charge of promotion.

When he talks I like to listen. And I think you will too, to this:

"We find at Macy's that the single most important thing in any advertisement which features merchandise—and almost all of ours do—is the merchandise itself. If it is something people don't want, or at a price they don't want to pay, there is little hope of getting an effective ad. The message can tell people about the virtue of a product, but it is an illusion to think it can substitute for lack of virtue.

"We find the second most important thing in our advertising is absolute honesty about what the merchandise really is. The customer who is led to believe too much by an advertisement is someone neither we, nor anyone, can afford for very long.

"Only third in importance is the contribution made by advertising itself; the form and excitement we can give the message through advertising techniques."

Once again let me say that advertising isn't magic; and the advertising business is not a game.

(The important thing to remember about the above is order. First comes the product: what it does, how well it does this and what it costs. Second is the promise: how carefully it is made and how truthfully. Third: how dramatically the product and its promise are presented. Change the order in your thinking and the advertisement will most likely fail.)

December 19

An item in the trade press tells of the appointment of *two* agencies to handle the promotion of a single product.

One is to handle publication advertising, the other radio and television.

And I wonder if this isn't bad for the advertiser, the agencies and the advertising business generally. Bad for the advertiser because neither agency can put against half the account the brains and the work that could be put to work on all of it. Bad for the agencies because success or failure can never be accurately measured and credited. And bad for the advertising business because the agencies involved may easily become trades people instead of professionals.

Who, for example, is going to decide how much of the advertising is to be in broadcasting and how much in print? If it is the advertiser, then the agencies simply are taking orders. If it is the agencies, then it is likely to be a compromise (and a nice, equitable split).

Split accounts by products are one thing. Split advertising *of* products is another. And I hope that Foote, Cone & Belding will never engage in it.

1952

January 2

1951 turned out to be a fairly busy year, according to my diary.

To begin with, I had 248 separate meetings with 572 individuals in our client organizations.

Trips out of town totalled 47 and included New York (25), Boston, Washington, Baltimore, Detroit, Dayton, Kansas City, Battle Creek, Neenah, Minneapolis, Denver, White Sulphur Springs . . . and London, Paris, Zurich and Bienne.

Days away from Chicago totalled 128, and nights on trains: 65.

Outside our own business, I acted as Chairman of the 4A's into April and as Chairman of The Advertising Council after April, as a Director of the AFA and a member of the Advertising Advisory Committee to the Secretary of Commerce, as a Director of The Community Fund of Chicago and The Chicago Association of Commerce and Industry, and as a Trustee of the University of Chicago and The Chicago Tumor Institute.

*

Incidentally, I attended 64 organized luncheons and 23 formal dinners (75 of which had practically the same menu).

January 3

Perhaps you will be interested in the following letter which I have sent to Sid Bernstein, editor of *Advertising Age* [In response to an article in the Dec. 31 issue reporting FC&B leading all agencies in number of vice-presidents]:

"While it is probably the most lighthearted, I can assure you that yours is not the first memorandum about advertising agency vice-presidents.

"Nor will it, I imagine, be the last.

"Over a long period of time a number of us in Foote, Cone & Belding have spent a great many hours on the subject. We have talked to other agencies. And for several years, at least in Chicago, we elected no new vice-presidents.

"Then, suddenly, we found ourselves in this position: some of our account groups were headed by vice-presidents, others—in every way similar, were not; certain of our accounts were supervised by vice-presidents, while others were not; some of our departments were headed by vice-presidents, while others, equally important, were not; finally, the distinction existed also in comparable positions in different offices.

"We had two choices if we wanted to be consistent. We could abolish the title. Or we could elect to vice-presidencies all those in similar positions to the then vice-presidents.

"We decided on the latter course. Our vice-presidents are the responsible members of the organization; they are responsible for the operation of our business for our clients, and they are responsible for the conduct of the business for the thousand-odd employees who live by it.

"In a partnership (as in a law office) these names would be listed in the letterhead—and no one, I believe, would think the number excessive in the case of any office.

"The thing is, we, like most agencies, operate as a corporation. There are many reasons for this.

"And so, while functioning along partnership lines— again, as in the case of the law firm, most agencies have come to the use of the corporate title, vice-president, to designate responsibility.

"In our own case, the vice-presidents are the people specifically responsible for our accounts, together with certain large-department heads.

"One reason why we may have more than some other agencies is because our offices in New York, Chicago, Los Angeles, San Francisco and Houston are complete agency units. In addition, there is our Radio and Motion Picture office in Hollywood.

"The vice-presidents are, in effect, the 'partners'.

"And we don't know any better way to designate them."

January 16

The tabulation is finished of my survey of Foote, Cone & Belding Chicago's people. And here is the composite picture:

Fifty-four per cent of us are women, forty-six per cent, men. Our women average a little under 30 years of age, our men, a little more than 35.

Seventy-two per cent of the men and sixty-four per cent of the women have had some college education; with 42 per cent of the former and 20 per cent of the latter being graduates.

Sixty-nine per cent of the men and twenty-five per cent of the women are married; another 4 per cent of men and 5 per cent of women have been. Seventy-nine per cent of the married men have families with children, twenty-seven per cent of the married women. Only 8 of us are grandparents. . . .

Life is the favorite magazine of 62 per cent of the men and 45 per cent of the women. *Time* is second with both, with 44 and 29 percent respectively. *The New Yorker* beats out the *Saturday Evening Post* for third place with men (33.3) and *Reader's Digest* (22.6) wins over *The New Yorker* with women. The best any woman's magazine can do with our women is 15 per cent (for the *Journal*) and *True* gets only 5 per cent and *Esquire*, 2 per cent of our men's votes. . . .

88 per cent of the women read books regularly, 94 per cent of the men. 65 per cent of the former and 81 per cent of the latter own television sets. And 75 per cent of men and 25 per cent of women own automobiles. . . .

Eighty per cent of our men and sixty per cent of women smoke, and 85 per cent of the men and 68 per cent of the women drink spirits.

*

I would think that we are pretty normal except for one thing. Only one person "doesn't know" what department he is in.

I am sure this is a record for a group of something over three hundred and fifty people (the number who answered the questionnaire).

(Little did I dream that thirty years later ninety per cent of our girls would be wearing skirts six inches above the knee.

And a similar percentage of our male artists and writers and television producers hair down to the shoulders fore and aft.)

February 5

It was only a question of who, I suppose, would be first to copy the dramatic huge-cake-without-plate-or-background layouts that have characterized the Pillsbury Mix advertisements of the last two or three years.

The dubious honor goes to Spry (*Chicago Tribune Graphic*, February 3).

And as always happens in such cases, the duplication of the Pillsbury appeal makes the page a Pillsbury page to every casual observer.

Thus, while I imagine the Pillsbury people and their agency (Burnett) are hot as hell at the steal, they really should be philosophic.

The Spry money is undoubtedly going to help Pillsbury more than Spry, and sooner or later Spry will back away and leave the huge cakes to their rightful owner—having paid an enormous price for their use.

When Kaffee Hag (decaffeinated coffee) followed exactly the appeal and the format of the Sanka magazine ads, readership studies showed that most people thought they *were* Sanka ads.

Result: Kaffee Hag went down and down in sales, finally sold its name to Sanka, and went quietly out of business.

May 13

I think it can now be said that the twentieth century has reached its zenith.

Sunday, on the TV broadcast of the baseball games, Chesterfield featured a special holiday package for Mother's Day!

June 17

There has recently been a great deal written on the subject of speculative work by agencies in competition for accounts, and much of the discussion has had to do with ethics.

However, until advertising is recognized as a profession, I think the question of ethics in invitational speculative presentations is somewhat beside the point.

On the other hand, I am convinced that professional status

will be achieved much sooner, to the benefit of all business, if the agencies decline to make such presentations—purely on economic grounds.

The fact is that speculative presentations cost money—lots of money in most cases, and if it is money well spent for the single successful speculator, it is sheer loss for each of the speculators who is unsuccessful. Moreover, the cost in the long run must be shared by the agencies' clients out of the time and effort and interest of people ordinarily assigned to them who are temporarily transferred to the speculative activity.

None of this is very good business for anyone. For sooner or later, if the practice becomes standard, every agency and every advertiser must pay the same price.

Since thousands of satisfactory agency appointments have been made, and hundreds more are made yearly, on the basis of agency current performance, personnel, facilities and operational procedure, and the character and interests of agency principals, I think that speculative competitions are—on the record, an unwarranted expense.

Foote, Cone & Belding will continue to have no part in these.

(Successful speculators maintain that the only unwarranted expense comes from unsuccessful speculation. But the fact remains that for every winner there are several losers. The worst loss is in the agencies' credibility with their own people.)

July 15

Perhaps the commercials got a little bit tedious and maybe the commentators commented at times unnecessarily, but I think these were only minor defects; the television of the Republican National Convention was a magnificent achievement.

More than this it was enormously significant. It showed up the wornout machinery and the antics and the shabby people of old-fashioned politics. And it set up some standards for new ones.

It is doubtful if the Democratic National Convention can meet these with only a week to prepare, but this is almost beside the point.

As television ownership spreads—so that all the people of America can see and hear the arguments and see who makes these and how, and who stands with whom—every man and wo-

man in political life will be accountable for the first time to an
informed public.

Television is the most powerful of all our means of communication. No other one even remotely approaches it.

*

It just might be noted too, that television will be no less
demoralizing to the buffoonery of advertising than it was last
week to that of politics.

*(I may have been a little too sanguine about the elimination
of buffoonery in television advertising. However, television has
so devastatingly exposed the political conventions for the farce
they are that their discontinuance is now fully predicted.*

*(For one thing, without the antics, the conventions are
dreadfully dull. Not even the best of the commentators can make
seconding speeches and roll calls exciting.)*

July 17

Procter & Gamble, maker of Ivory Soap, Dreft, Tide, Duz,
Oxydol, Cheer, Joy, Spic & Span, Lava, Camay, Drene, Prell,
Shasta, Lilt and Crisco, has begun an institutional advertising
campaign that could be pretty instructive.

For instance, P&G could explain how Drene, Prell and
Shasta *each* can give the one best shampoo; how Ivory and Camay *each* can promise the loveliest complexion; how Duz, Oxydol and Cheer *each* can get clothes whiter and brighter (presumably, than the others) ; and finally how Tide can guarantee
whiter, brighter washes than any *soap* while American Family
soap flakes (another P&G product) guarantees to make clothes
whiter and brighter than any *no-rinse suds* (like Tide).

I would like to know the answers because I would like to
pass them on to some bitter critics of advertising ethics.

Right now these critics have me stumped.

*(Today the multiple brands of Procter & Gamble each
makes its own promise to a segment of its market [i.e., Liquid
Prell for soft hair, Head & Shoulders for dandruff control, etc.,
and the same with the P&G laundry soaps and detergents], with
only an occasional leap from good to best.*

*(This is known as market segmentation and it has proved
more effective than the shotgun approach in inducing sampling
of improved products as well as new ones.)*

August 27

Back at the time of the Republican convention there appeared in *Life* and *Time* magazines an advertisement that I thought was one of the worst I had ever seen.

A rather large illustration showed a figure of Uncle Sam kneeling in prayer, and the headline read "America on its knees."

The text was a prayer to "Our Father in heaven . . . to save us from ourselves . . . to forgive us and help us, and finally, to fill us with new faith, new strength and new courage . . . to save us, before darkness falls."

The advertisement was signed by Conrad Hilton, president of the Hilton Hotels; and a dozen bright people with whom I talked agreed with me that the ad was in the worst possible taste.

Now I have seen the Starch report for the issue of *Life* that carried this monstrosity, and it is written here that more people—more men and women—read this advertisement than any other in the book.

Maybe there's a lesson in this. Or maybe it only helps to explain why "King Kong" is the Number One movie of the moment.

September 9

An article entitled *The Language of Advertising* in *Fortune,* for September, has a good deal to say that is sound about the use of stock expressions and advertising cliches, both of which it properly decries.

There is nothing here that is new, but there are a number of things that are often forgotten.

Perhaps most important is this: that there is no such thing as a Mass Mind. The Mass Audience is made up of individuals, and good advertising is written always from one person to another. If the promise that is held out to this one person is direct and worth while, it follows that it will be seized upon by others who may similarly benefit.

Thus—and only thus, does advertising move millions. When it is aimed at millions it rarely moves anyone.

October 14

A note on the infallibility of the press.

"In the ad agencies along Manhattan's Madison Avenue" (according to *Time,* October 13) "the true test of a huckster's sincerity is the way he speaks the language. But it is not the English language as most people know it; it is the adman's jargon, which changes as fast as a sponsor's mind when the Hooperating slumps. An adman who wants to keep 'with it' must change his vocabulary almost every week. Otherwise, he simply will not be considered an 'acute citizen'; he just won't be 'attuned.' Last week the acute citizen had some sharp new phrases:

"The office, once known as the 'shop,' is now the 'foundry,' 'store' or 'delicatessen.' An adman attends 'brainstorm sessions' instead of meetings; there, ideas are 'pressure cooked,' 'housebroken,' or merely 'kicked around.' And if no single idea is 'bought'—that is, if nobody 'gets any nourishment from it'—chances are a bunch of ideas will be 'Burbanked,' i.e., combined into a hybrid. At such high-level 'spitballing sessions' it may be advisable to 'pitch up a few mashie shots to see how close we are to the green.' Then, having made sure that the scheme has sufficient 'protein,' i.e., is a good idea, the proper people can be 'bulletined' and the deal 'team-worked' through.

"Any successful adman nowadays must 'get into the field'—even if it is only on a 'one-man survey'—to 'check the trade' and get an 'on-the-ground approach' to the 'big picture.' That means, of course, both 'sales-wise' and 'production-wise.' Then, having gotten a 'fill-in' (which is known in advertising circles as letting an outside dope in on the inside dope), he will be all set to 'finalize his thinking' and 'explode the market.' "

The word "shop" for office is one that I have heard used by men in every kind of business and "get into the field" is generally accepted as being pretty good practice in every line.

For the rest *Time* either is hitting the pipe or Madison Avenue is ten thousand miles from Park Avenue or Michigan Boulevard—for in all my travels I have never heard an advertising man use any other item in this crazy lexicon.

November 25

The following from Jim Felton (Los Angeles) comments on my recent quoting of *Time's* report on advertising jargon:

"*Time's* preoccupation with 'the adman's jargon' stems from *Time's* own thicket of journalese. As one who crawled out of this, bramble by bramble, I can recall every thorn in the *Time*-worn language of Rockefeller Center.

"For example, a *Time* correspondent does not interview a man. He 'brain-picks' him. He does not write a biographical sketch, or a personality story—he prepares a 'bioperse'. If it is good, he receives telegrams that may read: 'Kudos and congrats on dreamboat bioperse.' Dreamboat, of course, is about the finest story in the magazine, and, to the best of my knowledge originates from the vehicle a *Time* writer travels during the five days he writes a story.

"The magazine's own editing should be conclusive proof of its own jargon. But the halls of *Time* echo with a unique jabberwocky which, by comparison, would make the worst movie characterization of a Huckster sound like Winston Churchill.

"*Time* is not a magazine. It's a 'book'. 'What are you knocking out this week?' 'TS has me in the back of the book.' (TS was Thomas S. Mathews, the managing editor. 'Back of the book' included such departments as Books, Radio, Religion, Cinema, etc., which were edited earlier than 'front of the book' sections . . . National Affairs and Foreign Affairs.) 'When did you leave USAW?' (USAW was the war-time title of National Affairs—U. S. At War.) 'Last weekend.' (Week-ends at *Time* are Tuesday and Wednesday, the two days when the staff is not working.) 'I'm hoping to get into Biz but I've got to wait until Jones goes back to the field on his grass-roots junket.'

"Occasionally, those who enjoyed writing and reading English would discuss the lives of our *Time*. They would fill a great novel, or make a fine play. But our conclusion was always the same. No one would believe what they read or saw. A true portrayal of *Time's* editorial operation, the people who constitute it, the language they speak, their working habits, their 'pratfalls'—a great little item from *Time* jargon—would be, to others, an obvious exaggeration.

"Do you remember the *New Yorker* story in 1945 about *Time's* editorial masthead? It likened it, from bottom to top, to the intellectual alps, the peak towering above peak. The job titles are ridiculous enough. (Talk about our vice-presidents. Look at *Time's* editors.) But the most amusing thing to me about *Time's* masthead is the name Peter Matthews, listed under 'Contributing Editors'. This name has always appeared in the masthead. Always under the same heading. Poor fellow, he just does not seem to prosper or progress. And there's a reason for this. There is no Peter Matthews. *Time* lists him so that whenever some irate reader or advertiser complains about a story—so we were told—the front office can say: 'That goddam Peter Matthews. He wrote that story. We'll fire him tomorrow.' And, for the next few weeks, the line of type containing Peter Matthews' name would be deleted, only to reappear, for similar purposes, after the unhappy reader had been placated.

"Yet a magazine self-conscious enough to carry a fictitious name in its list of editors has the temerity to point a slanted pen at 'the adman's jargon.' "

1953

January 30

This is a memorandum to our Chicago copywriters and art directors.

I think that a good many advertising people today are "making ads" instead of trying to sell somebody something.

They are shouting when their tone should be conversational and they frequently wear Mexican Army uniforms when honest blue serge would suit better.

I want to break the rules of advertisingese and write plain English and set in plain type and illustrate our messages with catalogue integrity and usefulness.

Because I think we can have a lot of fun doing this and reap a huge reward for our clients as a result, I'm going to be looking for some changes and I think they may be quietly dramatic.

Here is how I propose that we go about this—fanatically:

1) Let us make every advertisement that we make as easy to understand and to appreciate as we know how—no matter how long this takes, nor how many cute ideas we have to throw away. First, let us make it as easy as we can for the reader to get our message. And, second, let us make these messages worth getting; let us tell the reader something that is important to that reader.

2) Let us make every advertisement that we make *personal*. Let us aim it at *one* person, just as we would in face-to-face contact; let us write it as if we were writing to a skeptical aunt,

and illustrate it as plainly. (All the rest of the world can look over our aunt's shoulder.)

3) Let us make our headlines point to our illustrations or explain them; make them work for each other. If we don't do this, either the headline or the illustration would seem to be unnecessary.

4) Let us be sure that our illustrations *are* illustrations, and not decorations or symbols. This is as much the writer's job as the artist's: to think of the advertisement as a whole, to know what each part is for.

5) Let us make our text advance the story and the sale—until it is complete. But let us make every word count, leaving out all that do not (including all of the superlatives and most of the adjectives).

6) Let us make our text as earnest and straightforward as our headlines (remember the skeptical aunt: what does she get out of our promise?). And let us use subheads or following illustrations wherever they will help.

7) Let's remember that if we could get it we would rather have a picture and caption and quick story in *Life* or the *Reader's Digest,* or a picture-and-caption story in *Better Homes & Gardens* than almost any ad ever written.

Let us remember this every time we make an ad and see how close we can come to it.

*

All this, if you please, is no more than pure Claude Hopkins. But a lot of people have got a long way away from it. And I think we can make all of our advertising (print and TV alike) much more exciting simply by coming a good part of the way back.

The only difference, really, would be in better (harder-working) illustrations made in almost documentary style.

*

I'm going to be watching, hard, and if we come out as I think we will—a lot of other people will be watching, too.

March 24

I have talked a good many times in recent months about impact in advertising. And I am very well aware that this may seem to be just one of those words that finds its way into this business from time to time — has its little heyday; then slips back into the language to languish forgotten.

But I think this is not the case with impact, for it has always been important in advertising.

The difference is, it has to come quicker today.

Indeed I believe that where once upon a time a newspaper or magazine campaign could develop considerable impact over a period of weeks or months, this is now impossible in many lines.

Radio made the job harder for all advertisers by greatly increasing the total amount of advertising to which the public was subjected.

With the growth of radio advertising, magazine and newspaper advertising increased enormously too.

Now there is television advertising added to radio, magazine, newspaper, outdoor, car card . . . and direct mail.

And for each advertiser in most lines in 1940 there are two or three or more in 1953.

Today, for example, Frigidaire (the traditional leader in refrigeration) faces *stiff* national advertising competition not only from General Electric and Kelvinator, but also from Westinghouse, Admiral, Philco, Crosley, Hotpoint, Norge, Coolerator, Deepfreeze, International Harvester, and locally from Sears' Coldspot.

In the current issue of *Better Homes & Gardens,* Frigidaire advertising must compete with that of Admiral, Coolerator, Crosley, Deepfreeze, General, Kelvinator, Norge, Philco and Servel —all in a welter of 414 pages.

In the shortening business in this same issue of *Better Homes & Gardens,* Spry must compete not only with Crisco, but also with Wesson Oil and Kraft Oil (in a double page spread). Softasilk competes with Swansdown, Gold Medal and two different kinds of Pillsbury cake flour or mix.

In addition, each of these products has also the relentless pressure of advertising from these and other similar products in other current magazines and other media.

Thus, it seems to me, the matter of impact is hardly academic. Impact is imperative—in campaigns and in single advertisements or radio or TV commercials. It is imperative, and I think it must be immediate.

For one thing, and I doubt if it is necessary to list any more, normal people simply haven't time to compare most products through advertising.

There are too many products and there is too much advertising.

The moral of all this is in three parts:

1) Let us be interesting (in our readers' or listeners' own interests).

2) Let us be quick.

3) Let us make our clients' advertising unmistakably theirs.

Let us think in terms of telegrams rather than letters—for a nation that is fast getting away from unnecessary work of *every* kind, including (if I am not mistaken) reading or listening to advertising.

If we can't be exciting—which I doubt—let us at least get down to the bone—in every ad and every commercial in every campaign for every client in our house.

And let us start today!

Let us give our advertising impact and, if I may start a new theme, let us also give it *urgency*.

Beginning this minute, I am going to check all of our production on this basis.

April 2

To Account Management, Art and Copy Departments:

One of the best demonstration commercials that I have ever seen on television appeared on the Goodyear Playhouse program last Sunday night.

It explained what happens when a tire blows out. And I won't forget it.

Nor will I forget that having made this demonstration — and shown graphically and reasonably how Goodyear tubes prevent blowout accidents, the scene dissolved into one in which a cutie SANG the Goodyear signoff in as silly a jingle as ever went over the air.

I urge you to look for this two weeks hence and review a lesson which could be entitled: "Mixing techniques is like mixing drinks and the result is apt to be poisonous."

July 22

You will be interested in the story behind the announcement of our appointment, last Thursday, by S. C. Johnson & Son, Inc.

In one way it is a very short story. In another it is a long one.

On Friday, May 22, we had a call from Mr. Stuart Watson, Johnson's advertising manager,* who explained his company's decision to appoint a second agency, and said they would like to talk with us.

Ten days later, [we] presented our case to Johnson's Mr. Fred Farwell, executive vice-president; Mr. Ray Carlson, marketing vice-president, and Mr. Watson, in a session here that lasted some five hours.

On Friday, June 19, Mr. Webber and I called on Mr. Watson, in Racine, with the list of our people who would be assigned to the Johnson account if this agency were chosen.

On Thursday, July 9, Messrs. Farwell, Carlson and Watson met with our designated group in Chicago.

And on Tuesday, July 14, after a meeting with Mr. Johnson in Racine, our appointment was announced.

This is the short story. And the Johnson people initiated the action.

But behind it all is the long story of doing good work for good people over many years, and of holding to a single standard of performance — even to the point of resigning a very large account . . .

(*Now president of Heublein.)

August 19

A recent piece of mine, in *Advertising Age,* has caused G. & C. Merriam Company, Publishers, to practically promise a revision in the next edition of Webster's New Collegiate Dictionary.

I objected to the use of the word *meretricious* as applied to broadcasting for commercial purposes under the definition of the word *huckster.*

(The Merriam people were as good as their word. They no longer classify broadcast advertising as being necessarily insincere.)

November 17

That personal salesmanship is at a low level of effectiveness is hardly news. The trade press is full of lamentation and the wailing of sales managers is loud and prolonged. The fact seems to be that the vast majority of salesmen today simply can't (or won't) sell. The only advantage they accept for their products is a price advantage, and they have come to demand this in increasing numbers.

One result has been an avalanche of dealing—one-cent sales, coupons, give-aways and what not—with the end result that there are products in more than a few categories that can only be sold in quantities at cut prices.

Another is that more and more advertising has come to be aimed at the salesman and his trade instead of at the consumer —the group for whom advertising was invented, and the only group that can make it effective over any long period of time.

I can think of no greater waste than buying thousands of dollars' worth of space and time and filling it primarily for a few hundred salesmen and their trade. Yet this happens every day. "The salesmen don't like it," has sounded the death knell for many a good consumer campaign.

Now one can only ponder the question: What is it in the makeup of an average salesman (who works only with the trade) that makes his opinion on consumer advertising so much more important than that of trained, experienced advertising people?

When I hear of a poll of salesmen to decide where to locate a plant or how much to spend to build one or how it shall be designed, then I shall believe that their opinions on advertising, too, should be sought.

Until I do, I shall thank God that most of our clients still put advertising on a professional basis to sell demonstrably good products at fair prices to huge groups of people; to move goods off shelves and showroom floors, and not to put them on.

The latter is the salesman's job; and he can do it continuously only in ratio to the effectiveness of consumer advertising —done straight.

1954

July 26

This is as serious a memorandum as I have ever dictated. I have been thinking a great deal about Herman Lehman's continuing insistence that Frigidaire advertising be fighting advertising.

The fact is that appliances today are offered for sale by thousands of store operators who do little or no hard selling for any manufacturer. They give the customer what he or she wants; if they haven't got it in stock, they get it; they don't argue.

And so it is that the hard sell—the fight for the sale, must be made in advertising. There is simply no other way to put a make or brand across, and to maintain it—against lower prices and deals and special offers . . . and, most of all, the lack of loyal, vigorous salesmanship at retail.

The challenge is now put squarely up to advertising. And I believe that, increasingly, this is a challenge not only to leadership but, actually, to survival.

Moreover, it is not confined to the appliance field.

Our advertising has to fight for every product in the house and it has to fight smart and fast as well as hard. We have to be alert to what each competitor for each of our products is doing every day. We have to know what he is saying and where he is saying it and how often.

We have to meet him and beat him. Or he will beat us.

August 24

Advertising, like everything else, changes.

The agency's domestic volume for the first seven months of 1953 totalled $34,952,000; omitting art and preparation, 60% of this was in magazines and newspapers, 10% in outdoor, 15% in radio, and 15% in television.

In the first seven months of 1954, magazines and newspapers declined to 57%, outdoor to 7%, and radio to 10%, while television increased to 26% of the considerably larger total of $40,256,000 . . .

October 15

One of the constant pressures in this and, I suppose, every advertising agency, is the demand for new names for new products. And nothing is more disheartening. For every time we propose an appropriate new name, it turns out that somebody in some place like Antioch, Cal., or Baton Rouge, La., or Van Wert, O., has been using it for years for a local product, and we can't have it.

I am reminded that even when Jack Platt attempted, perhaps in jest, to clear the first part of the first name of Kraft's president, Mr. Grellett Pound, for Kraft's new dog food, he discovered that Grell had long been registered in a number of fields including this one!

This, and our own most recent experience with names for salad dressing and insecticide, causes me to look with considerable interest at the A&P which apparently has said: "To hell with making sense."

The Tea company is advertising *Little-Bo-Peep* Ammonia.

(Before Henry Ford II chose the name Edsel for his new automobile in 1957, we submitted 6,000 alternates. All better.)

December 20

Here are some items that are a little outside the field of the Census, but not, I think, too far to be noted along with the usual data.

They come from George Gallup's staff, and I copied them out of *Time:*

"Out of 102 million U. S. adults, approximately half have visited Chicago and New York City. About 5.5 million men have been to London, 6.5 million to Paris— a large percentage of them by courtesy of the U. S. armed forces.

"Ten million women and 7.5 million men have read the Bible all the way through.

"Eleven million men and 10 million women have written their Congressmen.

"Slightly more than half the adult population have eaten lobsters.

"Some 62% of all men and 27% of the women have played poker for money; 17 million men and 11 million women have bet money at a race track.

"Half of all U. S. men have had a fist fight since they were 15, but only one woman in ten has engaged in a hair-pulling match. Seventeen percent of men admit they have hit their wives, and 18% of women say they have struck their husbands.

"A total of 32 million men and 10 million women have gone swimming in the nude.

"Eighteen million Americans have seen Harry Truman in person.

"Nineteen million have gone hungry for lack of money.

"Half of American adult males and third of females have stayed out all night on a party.

"Ten million men and 4,000,000 women have pawned something in their lifetime.

"Some 28.5 million men and 11.5 million women claim they have caught a fish weighing more than two pounds.

"Twenty percent of all women and 8% of the men have been telephoned on a radio-TV quiz."

I think there are some things there for advertising people to ponder.

1955

April 5

In an interview in the current issue of *Printers' Ink,* Alfred Politz, having mentioned sex appeal in advertising, was asked whether, in his opinion, this is something that should be worked into *all* advertising—and I like his answer:

"I do agree with Freud that sex is the basic underlying drive that motivates all mankind. *No,* I do not believe that it is necessary (or most effective) always to ring in a sex appeal.

"Sex is like gravity. Everything we do is affected by gravity. You could not drive a car if it were not for gravity keeping the car from flying off into space. But there is no point in talking about gravity in a radio commercial about an automobile.

"Everything we do is affected by our sex drive. We could not have babies to feed if it were not for the sex drive. But it is not necessary to use a sex appeal specifically to sell baby food."

(The proverbial man from Mars, viewing television, might easily conclude that sex is not only our national pasttime, having taken the place of baseball, but also our number one item for exploitation.

(The zenith [or perhaps I should say the nadir] was

*reached when Joe Namath, the footballer, became the latest sex
object in U. S. advertising.)*

April 19

Probably the worst waste in current printed advertising is
the vast number of pages and spreads that attempt to gain impact simply by using large illustrations and/or large type.

Impact, if I am not mistaken, is only important when it is
selling impact. And *Life,* this week, for example, is filled with
impact-planned advertisements that are almost devoid of selling
ideas. The result is principally that the pages shout for little or
no reason and the effect is merely tiresome . . .

The fact is, the enormous total weight of advertising today
makes compelling ideas, selling ideas, more important than ever
before. The dearth of these, it seems to me, offers us an opportunity against most competitive products that rarely has been
so great.

What we must ask ourselves of every piece of copy and
every layout is *what does it promise and what does it prove?*
And then, of course, *should anyone really care?*

If we can't answer the last question affirmatively, and posi-
tively, we'll only be following some very bad examples.

Perhaps a further test should be: *how would this look, how
would this sound, in TV?*

June 6

Last Thursday we had a meeting in Dayton wherein Milton
Schwartz presented our announcement campaign for the 1956
line of Frigidaire appliances.

This was the most completely planned and integrated and
scheduled campaign that has ever been presented to Frigidaire,
and the result was enthusiastic approval.

This is to say thank you to the large number of people who
participated in the several months of activity that ended some
time in the middle of the night before Thursday's presentation.

[The memo concluded with the names of 57 FC&B people
and four outside companies who participated.]

*(Ten weeks later, on Aug. 19, Frigidaire announced its
account was being given to Kudner Agency, after 20 years with
FC&B and its predecessor. The move was a particular surprise
because five weeks previously, Frigidaire disbanded its own pro-*

*motion staff and added responsibility for its $6,000,000 annual
investment to the $10,000,000 space budget administered by
FC&B.*

*(No satisfactory explanation has ever been given for the
switch which was as much a surprise to Jim Ellis, head of Kudner, as it was to me. Ellis had never been in Dayton prior to the
day his company was appointed.*

*(We may simply have been part of a general house cleaning
instituted by a new General Motors official in charge of the Dayton properties. If so, our termination followed the classic sweep
of the new broom.*

(It came as a shock nevertheless.)

July 6

There are so many new people in the company that I would
like to make a point to them that I think is not always under-
stood in advertising.

The sum total today—of both time and space advertising—
is so great that no ordinary ideas have a chance to get through;
one more little voice only adds to the babel.

And so we must think and plan to make our advertising
different from our competitors', and keep it so. We must remember that it is neither big type nor big words nor big pictures,
but big ideas that make advertising successful; big ideas that
make honest promises clear and commanding.

This little memo is written by chance on Independence Day,
but my hope is constant that there is nothing compulsory about
the way we are presently doing anything — except thinking
freely, for our clients.

In recent weeks I have seen some exciting and powerful new
campaigns for several of our clients, both Chicago and New
York, and I trust that we will continue to break every old rule
save only the one to show our prospects why it is in their own
best selfish interests to buy the goods we have to sell.

The thing is, there is always more than one way to do this.
And we have to find, if we can, the most compelling way . . .

August 24

I suppose it is inevitable that in the next several weeks we
will all hear stories and rumors about the effect of the Frigidaire defection upon our business now and in the future. There
will be fine, big crocodile tears shed for us.

And none of this will make any difference.

Consider this fact: If all of the accounts that have been removed through the years from J. Walter Thompson Company, for instance, were totaled up they would probably represent a volume larger than any other agency's today.

What is perhaps much more important is that we shall now be eligible for a number of accounts—several of which we have in the past found it necessary to decline because of our General Motors connection.

(Within hours, almost, of the announcement of our termination by Frigidaire, we received an invitation from Ford to solicit the advertising for a new car to be introduced two years hence.

(The new car was the ill-fated Edsel, for which we were appointed after what was probably the fiercest competition in advertising history.

(My own account of this appears in With All Its Faults, *Little, Brown and Company, Boston—1969.)*

September 13

I think you will be more than casually interested in a memorandum written by David Ogilvy to Jim McCaffrey* of Ogilvy, Benson & Mather, a few weeks ago, and sent out to the agency's prospects. David Ogilvy's rise to fame began with the "Man in the Hathaway Shirt" (the man with the eye patch):

"I am better at making campaigns than at pontificating about theory, but here are twelve things I believe about the creative side of our job:

"1. Every advertisement is a part of the long-term investment in the personality of the brand.

"2. If your campaign is not built around a BIG IDEA, it will be second class.

"3. In advertising, the beginning of greatness is to be *conspicuous* and *different*. The beginning of failure is to be *invisible* and *orthodox*.

"4. In advertising, compromise is oblivion. Whatever you do, *go the whole hog*.

"5. Play your selling theme loud and clear—so everyone can see it *at a glance*.

"6. The average person reads only *four* advertisements in the average magazine. Advertisements can't sell if nobody reads them. You can't save souls in an empty church.

"7.   You cannot *bore* consumers into buying your product. It is better to *interest* them in buying it.

"8.   The consumer is not a moron. She is *your wife*. And she is grown-up.

"9.   Our advertisements tell the truth, but we *make the truth exciting*.

"10.   Good salesmen are *inexorable* but *charming*. So are good advertising campaigns. It pays to be *friendly*.

"11.   No good campaign was ever continued too long, and no good advertisement was ever repeated too often.

"12.   It is never too late to *improve* an advertisement— even *after* the client has OK'd it."

(*Jim McCaffrey is now a principal in the McCaffrey & McCall advertising agency in New York. Ogilvy, Benson & Mather is now Ogilvy & Mather, still headed by the ineffable David Ogilvy, who has built one of the most distinguished of contemporary agencies.)

1956

March 22

Art in Advertising for January contains the following from one of my favorite advertising people, Mr. David Ogilvy.

It is entitled "What Every Young Art Director Should Know" and it is subheaded "A 30-Point Cram-Course."

"Don't be led astray by the highbrows in your ranks.

"These misguided fellows do your profession a disservice. They foster the impression—all too widely held— that art directors as a class are indifferent to considerations of 'business'.

"Awards juries, dominated by these highbrows, give prizes to advertisements whose only distinguishing feature is their debt to Mondrian or Paul Klee. It is as if copywriters were to band together and give awards for advertisements written in the manner of Gertrude

Stein; what effect do you suppose that would have on the status of the copywriting profession?

"The highbrow minority among art directors cares little about research. They know nothing about the factors which really make advertisements succeed or fail. Unfortunately, many art schools are infested with teachers whose knowledge of modern advertising techniques is equally limited. They do incalculable damage to the careers of their students.

"For example, many of them teach you to use type for purposes of *decoration*—an appalling crime, in that it reduces readership.

"They also teach you to use *art work* in advertisements sublimely unaware of the fact that, in nine cases out of ten, *photographs* attract more readers, and sell more merchandise.

"On the assumption that you, gentle reader, have only recently escaped from the clutches of just such ignorant teaching, I now offer you a 30-point cram-course in the eternal verities of art direction:

"1. The *subject* of your photograph is more important than your choice of photographer. Content is more important than technique. One great subject can make you famous.

"2. Don't rely on copywriters to think up the subjects for your photographs. Set your own imagination to work, morning, noon and night. Concentrate on the kind of subject which will make the reader say to himself: *'What goes on here?'* Try to arouse *curiosity*.

"3. Photographs which contain a strong element of *story* are the best. 'Art' photographs, the kind that win prizes in camera clubs, are not successful in advertising—they don't work *fast* enough.

"4. It is better to have one central figure in your photograph—a hero or heroine, as it were—than a group of two or three.

"5. The bigger the photograph, the more readers will stop and read the copy. Better one big picture than two small ones.

"6. When you use color photographs, rich dark tones stop more readers than light high-key tones.

"7. Historical illustrations are always a flop.

"8. When you use bleed (and I advise you to do so as often as you can) *make the most of it*. Bleed your main photograph on three sides. You get a bigger audience that way.

"9. Always be literal, realistic, simple, and direct. Never be symbolic, complex, obscure or indirect. Readers have a genius for missing the point; they are in a hurry.

"10. Learn to *draw*. An art director who can't draw is like a salesman who can't talk—he just doesn't get his ideas across. Few account executives or clients have enough visual imagination to understand what you mean unless you draw well—or use scrap photographs.

"11. Bone up on typography. Most young art directors are so scandalously ignorant on this subject that management is obliged to buttress them with expensive specialists. Learn to specify your own type—emancipate yourself from dependence on typographers.

"12. The typography in advertisements should never be self-conscious or obtrusive. The object of type is to make it as easy as possible for the readers to read what the copywriter has written. Don't let your own idiosyncracies get in the way.

"13. Don't allow copywriters to use more than twelve words, or one sentence, in the first paragraph. Keep all sentences and all paragraphs *short*.

"14. Break up the monotony of long copy by setting some paragraphs in bold face, some in italic, some underscored, some indented. Use initial letters, numbering, arrow-heads, bullets and asterisks to get readers into the copy.

"15. Insist on your copywriter providing you with plenty of crossheads for long copy ads.

"16. Never square-up your paragraphs. Widows are the breath of life.

"17. Never use a sans-serif face for body copy. Readers are not accustomed to it.

"18. Never use reverse-plate. It reduces reading 50 per cent.

"19. Never set any type over your illustration—or over a tint.

"20. Never use more than two type faces in one advertisement. In most cases, one should be enough. When in doubt, use Caslon.

"21. Keep your layouts uncluttered with gadgetry.

"22. Always set type on an even keel—never slanting on the page.

"23. Always put a caption under every photograph. Captions are read by more people than body copy —that's why they are so important.

"24. In magazine advertisements, never rout out the background. In newspapers, be careful to avoid large areas of grey background.

"25. Before you submit your layout for OK, always look at it *in context*—in the medium in which it will appear. Paste it in the magazine or the newspaper. This practice will teach you a lot. (The public never sees advertisements matted and cellophaned.)

"26. When you get a new account, start by studying the precedents. You have a lot of problems to solve, but none of your problems are new. They have confronted other art directors, and most of them have been solved rather well. Don't be too hard-headed to learn from your predecessors or your peers.

"27. Watch what editors do. Generally speaking, editorial techniques outpull conventional advertising techniques.

"28. Subscribe to half a dozen foreign magazines— *Punch, Realities, Nouveau Femina,* etc. You can get stimulus, ideas and useful scrap from them.

"29. Spend at least two hours a week in an art gallery; and go to Europe every other year.

"30. If you don't like your job, get another one. 'Be

happy while you're living, for you're a long time dead.' "

(I have Mr. Ogilvy's gracious consent to reproduce the above two memoes and one yet to come exactly as they appeared. He wouldn't change a word. Nor would I.)

April 20

I have said all that I have it in mind to say about advertising's need for greater creativity in the face of the current annual volume of more than $9 billion.

However, there are a number of things about this creativity that I think it would be well to put down.

In the very first place, it should be perfectly clear that creativity in advertising is not a matter solely of words and pictures.

The marketing plan is essentially creative. Thus, if our account managers are not creative and if our research and merchandising people are not creative and if our media people are not creative, our words and pictures—however appropriate, will go for nothing.

Moreover, if our production people, for instance, are not creative in the development of new techniques of reproduction we will be getting something less than full value out of all our other effort before and after.

Creativity is the key to everything that we do well. Without it our work can only be satisfactory. And satisfactory in business is like the grade of "C" in school. It is just one step from *unsatisfactory*.

(Creativity has become, insofar as I am concerned, almost a dirty word. Too often it refers to kookie television commercials and to magazine and newspaper advertising that adopts the television pattern—hopefully to beguile the viewer rather than attract attention reasonably to a worthwhile proposition.

(Creativity as it is practiced today by many advertising people results in advertising for advertising people.

(How, then, can it succeed as some [if not all of it] does? The reason, I think, is because advertising today talks to so many people that it needs only a relatively small percentage of television's millions of viewers, for instance, to react favorably.

(Also, by constant dinning, the hard core sales proposition undoubtedly gets through to a good many people who will tell

you that they detest the foolish commercials and pay them no attention whatever.

(Truly creative advertising—as against today's improvisation in advertising—follows the rules for clarity and character that make people respect advertising for the information it contains.)

April 26

One of the things that has always annoyed most of us is to read the proxy statement of a corporation and find that many, if not most of its directors are very, very small stockholders.

I remember a company where I owned a few shares, a few years ago, where it turned out that I owned more, for some $8,000, than eleven of the fifteen directors of the company.

What brings this to mind is a proxy statement received this morning from the Ford Motor Company, and I think you will be interested in the very heavy ownings of almost all the directors in this company.

Indeed, of the thirteen directors, only the two who are outside directors own total shares worth less than a million dollars.

This, it seems to me, is the way it should be.

May 15

Shares in our various client companies traded on the New York Stock Exchange last Friday had a value of $2,864,403.

Armour	$ 88,175
Beatrice	4,825
Firestone	15,800
Ford	525,125
General Foods	46,300
Gillette (Paper-Mate)	108,399
Kimberly-Clark	133,125
Libby	53,229
Lockheed	91,675
Magnavox	131,175
Minneapolis-Honeywell	464,450
Montgomery Ward	335,350
National Dairy (Kraft)	113,100
Safeway	172,200

Schenley (Roma)	42,680
Southern Pacific	440,425
TWA	49,720
Hiram Walker	48,650
	$2,864,403

The shares bought each day represent faith on the part of hundreds of buyers that each is making a solid investment based on continuing sales and profits. To help to justify this faith is our responsibility. And planning and making *great* advertising alone will satisfy it.

May 22

Few writers have made the American language crackle as did H. L. Mencken, who currently is being rediscovered.

From the notes for future essays published last week under the title "Minority Report: H. L. Mencken's Notebooks" (Knopf), this week's *Time* culls a dozen samples.

For instance, Mencken wrote: "Experience is a poor guide to man . . . A man really learns little by it, for it is narrowly limited in range. What does a faithful husband know of women, or a faithful wife of men? The generalizations of such persons are always inaccurate. What really teaches man is not experience, but observation. It is observation that enables him to make use of the vastly greater experience of other men, of men taken in the mass. He learns by noting what happens to them. Confined to what happens to himself, he labors eternally under an insufficiency of data."

This is something more than an example of Henry Mencken's audacious use of accepted fact to prove the opposite. It is also the business of stimulating mental juices and Mencken can be a powerful stimulant.

Utter reliance on experience is a curse on all business.

A little of Mencken's contempt for it could make the ordinary advertising dish considerably more exciting.

May 24

The effectiveness of radio as a medium in this television age is seldom better illustrated than by the success of Pepsodent's heavy concentration of spots in one of the major markets reported by Nielsen.

Concurrent with the introduction and sampling of Procter & Gamble's new Crest fluoride tooth paste, Gleem in six months dropped 25% in sales, Colgate lost 20% of its volume, and Ipana 11% to the newcomer, while Pepsodent (You'll Wonder Where the Yellow Went) held steady.

August 29

I wish you would read these numbers, slowly and carefully, and note the asterisks between some of them.

5, 4, 6, 2, 2, 4, 4, 3, 1, 6, 5, 3, 1, 1, 1, 5, 1, 1, 3 * 7, 5, 1, 5 * 3, 7, 7, 3, 13, 2, 5, 3, 7, 1, 1, 3, 3 * 1, 9.

2, 2, 1, 3, 2, 1, 1 * 1, 4, 5, 3, 2, 1, 19, 9, 10, 3, 10, 3, 3, 13, 13, 6, 6, 5, 3, 2, 1, 1, 5, 3 * 2, 2, 2, 7 * 3, 2, 6, 7.

These are the Starch "read most" percentages first for men and second for women, for all the advertisements, ½ page or larger, with formal text, in the *Saturday Evening Post* for July 14, 1956. The asterisks indicate no reading at all.

The picture is the picture of our problem: to make printed advertising *worth reading* in the television era.

Before television even the higher of these figures were multiplied three and four and five times.

September 20

I continue to be concerned about the need of advertising to be more creative when there is a total of $10 billion involved as there is this year, than when there was only one-third as much, as was the case ten years ago.

The necessity grows greater almost by the week.

To illustrate this, the September 24 issue of *Life* has a double-page spread for almost every three one-page advertisements!

There are 63 page advertisements in the issue and 20 spreads.

Moreover, of the 63 page advertisers, only 13 use television; whereas, of the 20 advertisers in spreads, 9 use television.

There are two points to make. In the first place, the 63 page advertisers have a much harder job to make an impact than do the 20 spread advertisers. Second, the four-fifths of

the page advertisers who do not use television are even more
in need of outstanding creative effort than the half (almost)
of the spread advertisers who do use television and on a regular
schedule.

All this is some of the complication of advertising in 1956.

*(Here let me repeat that there is a vast difference between
creativity and mere improvisation.*

*(Retail advertising, which is rarely inspired, creates inter-
est which, in turn, creates sales, on a basis that more manufacturers should embrace. When they do this, relying on the news
and the values involved in their products rather than the very
latest advertising invention, the chances of their success are
much greater. Moreover, this works exceedingly well in print.)*

October 4

David Sarnoff, board chairman of Radio Corporation of
America, has said some of these things before. But I think his
prophesies are worth repeating.

Speaking at a dinner in his honor, in New York City last
Sunday, he said that as impressive as the developments of the
last century have been, "I am convinced that they will be
eclipsed by the events of the next twenty years."

He then predicted the following developments within those
years:

Nuclear energy will be both plentiful and economical,
not only for industry, but for planes, ships, trains and
automobiles.

The energy of sun rays will be effectively harnessed
and in worldwide use.

Communication by television, in full color, will be possible around the world. Individuals will be able to hold
private two-way conversations, and see each other as
they talk, regardless of the distance separating them.

Jet-propulsion and rocket-type vehicles, using nuclear
fuels, will travel at speeds as great as 5,000 miles an
hour.

Electronic light will bring startling new types of illu-
mination. It will provide light without heat, without
glare and almost without shadow.

Electronic computers will take over recording and accounting tasks, freeing for other work "the great majority of the nine million Americans now engaged in clerical tasks."

"The housewife's dream of an all-automatic home will be realized," Mr. Sarnoff said. "The day's chores in the home will be prescheduled, with each of the tasks performed electronically.

"Not only will the prediction of weather for months or even years ahead be perfected, but major steps will have been taken to make and control weather as desired."

(David Sarnoff, like Frank Stanton, has seen many of his prophecies come true.

(What neither dreamed of [or if he did he quickly forgot it like a nightmare] was the depletion of natural resources which is currently a matter of a great deal more concern than the future of the computer.)

October 9

Almost all of the myths about women have been promoted by men.

Generally we are told that women are more emotional than men. And this is supposed to take care of them.

However, according to an eminent anthropologist, Dr. Ashley Montague of Rutgers University, emotionality should never be confused with emotional stability. The male's stiff upper lip is no measure of the latter.

Woman is not only more intelligent than man (a female at five is two years ahead in intelligence—and maintains her advantage all through life) but also much more stable emotionally. She cries, but this is good. Woman's emotions are like shock absorbers; they are rarely denied, they work all the time to her benefit.

James Stephens, the poet, said: Women are wiser than men because they know less and understand more.

Perhaps this is why male mental casualties after two years of aerial bombardment in London during World War II, were carefully recorded by a British medical association as 70 to 1 over female casualties.

Male suicides in the U. S. outnumber the female 3 to 1.

The thing is: Are we talking to women in our advertising as they are (trying everything on for size, mentally) or are we talking to them as we think they are—pretty and soft, in a rough, tough, masculine world?

Consider that when the average (or normal) man leaves for work in the morning, for his job and lunch and his afternoon's work and getting home again, the woman has to plan two meals, get the children off to school, call the plumber, argue with the laundress, worry about the painting, the bad reception on Channel 2, the flowers for the party on Saturday night, the menu for same, see to the doctor, the dentist, Johnnie's bad grade in arithmetic, Julie's posture, the P.T.A. meeting, mice in the basement, the car pool for school, the roast that was tough, Julie's dresses that are getting too short, Johnnie's shoes that need repairing, the lessons for Sunday school, the music lessons, gas for the car, etc., etc.—*and* how she'll look and how she'll sound when the man gets home.

Think about it. And think how she'll look at our ads in the *Journal*. Or on television.

Remember, the woman's meanest job, aside from ironing, is meal planning (this from the editor of *BH&G*). But this is only one thing. The thing she wants most is her family's happiness; in it lies her own creative success.

Let us ask ourselves: do we understand her at all; are we really helping her?

Are we even trying?

Or are we only acting like men who know everything there is to know—and know almost nothing at all of what she is up against, sixteen hours a day, 365 days a year?

These are questions that were asked at the General Foods marketing meeting in New York on Friday.

December 4—Carmel, Cal.

I still am amazed at the whiskey advertising in the newspapers, the amount of it. And now I am beginning to be amazed also at the number of foolish advertisers who can only copy other advertisers. Just now you can't tell a Marlboro ad from a "21" brand whiskey ad from a Tareyton ad from a Schweppes ad from a Philip Morris ad from a Bellows ad from a Schenley ad; and this is dopey.

J. C. Doyle, general sales manager for the Edsel automobile, was quoted in yesterday's *San Francisco Examiner* as being very happy with the assignment of the advertising for the new car to Foote, Cone & Belding. "We found no hucksters there," he said.

December 27

The bucketsful of tears shed over the passing of *Collier's* and *Woman's Home Companion* from the scene tend to obscure an important fact. And so do the imprecations of Mr. Paul Smith, the president-publisher-editor, who is quoted in *Printers' Ink* as saying that "the group loosely defined as Madison Avenue pulled the rug" out from under the enterprise.

The fact is that *Collier's* fell far behind its competition in the years between the two world wars. *Life* and *Look* entered the lists with new appeals and new approaches and new editorial techniques that *Collier's* simply failed to match. Still worse, during the last ten years there have been at least five loud announcements of a "new" *Collier's* that never materialized. Only the names on the masthead changed. Actually, Smith and the newest editor, Ken McArdle, were finally bringing out a vastly improved magazine. But advertiser and agency alike had every reason to wait and see: the Crowell-Collier Publishing Company was a manufacturer which happened to manufacture magazines and there was no guarantee at all that it would stick to any course.

Personally, I am much more sorry about the demise of *Collier's* than about the colorless *Companion*. Several months ago I wrote a piece for *Collier's* and while I was paid, and paid well, for it, I mostly wanted to see it in print.

It was a defense of the advertising people who now are said to have killed the magazine.

(The demise of Collier's *marked the beginning of the end of an era that was dominated in publishing by the great weekly magazines—*Collier's, Saturday Evening Post, Look *(bi-weekly) and* Life. All but Collier's *died of a curious combination of greed and nearsightedness. The greed resulted in swollen circulation, millions of subscriptions obtained at astronomical cost and quite beyond the willingness of advertisers to pay for. The myopia that affected the editors and publishers of the* Post, Look *and* Life, *which expired in that order, made them ignore the growing power of television.*

(First they tried to fight it with circulation. Then they revamped their magazines to meet the threat editorially. But time

*defeated them. Television is instantaneous and you are there—
at whatever is projected on the little screen.*

*(The big weekly magazines were out of date when they were
issued. Besides, the interests of millions of people have become
special interests and the weeklies were general magazines.)*

December 31

Last week's issue of *Advertising Age* carried the most exhaustive coverage of the expenditures and advertising and
selling organizations of the 100 leading advertisers that anyone
has ever undertaken.

The figures estimated for our own clients are so close to
those we know that I can only assume the same accuracy of
compilation for the other advertisers, and the ever-changing
organizations by departments also are very nearly up to the
minute where I know these.

Advertising Age has put us all in its debt.

As I think you know, twelve of the 100 leading advertisers
are clients of this agency. These are General Foods, Ford,
Lever, National Dairy (Kraft), Gillette (Paper-Mate), Schenley (Roma), Armour, Walker, Johnson, Kimberly-Clark, Liebmann and TWA.

Of the top 25 newspaper advertisers, six are our clients:
Ford, General Foods, Lever, National Dairy, Armour and Walker. Of the top 25 in network television, six are our clients: Gillette, General Foods, Lever, Ford, National Dairy and Johnson.
Of the top 25 magazine advertisers, four are our clients: General Foods, Ford, Kimberly-Clark and National Dairy. Of the
top 25 in outdoor, five are our clients: Ford, General Foods,
Liebmann, National Dairy and Walker. In business publications
there are two: Armour and Kimberly-Clark. And in farm papers, one: Ford.

1957

March 12

All of us who took part in our several meetings with the
Allstate Insurance people are disappointed that they chose another advertising agency.

However, someone always has to be disappointed when an
advertiser makes a choice.

This happened to be a final decision between two agencies that have come down to the wire together before. Last time, in the solicitation for the Edsel account of the Ford Motor Company, we were successful over Leo Burnett Company.

This time Burnett won out.

Let's wish them and Allstate a long successful association.

April 26

If you want to know how far a good idea can go, look here.

Last summer, Don Williams had the idea that a song written about the Pepsodent jingle, "You'll Wonder Where the Yellow Went," could be promoted with disk jockeys across the country and might double the circulation of the paid advertising.

So he wrote a song.

Now the figures are in.

"You'll Wonder Where the Yellow Went" (Decca Record 29973-A) has been played locally 3,125 times and 298 times network for a total of 3,423 plays.

The question now is, would this have happened to any record?

The answer is no. The other side of Decca 29973-A is "A Frantic Antic." This was played 609 times locally and no times on network, for a total of 609.

Figuring the free air time for "You'll Wonder Where the Yellow Went" based on NBC major market time rates ($125 local—$13,000 network—for one minute spot) the total value was $4,264,625.

The total cost of the promotion was $6,675.

Don Williams thought I might find this interesting.

I think it is fantastic!

October 22

Two events of last week made television history.

One was the hour-long Edsel Show with Bing Crosby in his first live appearance, with Frank Sinatra, Rosemary Clooney and Louis Armstrong. *The New York Times* called this "a smash hit . . . the richest of entertainment" and some reviewers went so far as to say that it was the greatest of all popular programs.

The other event, four days later, was the revival of "Green Pastures" on the Hallmark Hall of Fame, of which the same

New York Times said, "Television last night had one of its most glorious evenings . . . a superb production . . . an unforgettable ninety minutes . . . a fine and glowing achievement."

Obviously, we can't reach such heights every time. But it is something to know that our television people never cease trying.

December 17

The announcement from Flint, Mich., that Kudner Advertising, Inc. has been terminated by the Buick Division, General Motors Corporation, should make everyone in advertising a little bit sad.

Through the years of Kudner direction (22), Buick advertising has ranged from some of the best in the automobile industry to some of the worst, loud and meaningless.

The facts must be fairly clear to any observer. Less and less acceptable Buick automobiles in each of the last several years have been advertised with more and more frantic appeals.

Finally these have become almost impossible. "New sweetheart of Sigma Chi," was a recent four-color magazine headline!

That any of this came voluntarily from Kudner is doubtful on the basis of Kudner performance for Fisher Body and General Motors (institutional), both of which have quality and substance.

It can only be that once again the failure of an unacceptable product has been blamed on badly dictated advertising.

December 31

Good wishes are not the only happy tidings that come in the year-end mails.

Within only a few days I have been extended all the privileges of the house—including credit, by the following hotels: the Commodore, Waldorf-Astoria, Plaza, Statler, Biltmore, Barclay, Savoy-Plaza, Gotham, Hampshire House, Warwick and Roosevelt, in New York City; the Parker House, Somerset and Statler, in Boston; the Drake, Ambassador East, Ambassador West, Sherman, Edgewater Beach, Conrad Hilton and Palmer House, in Chicago; the Statler in Detroit; the Beverly-Hilton, Beverly-Wilshire, Statler and Ambassador, in Los Angeles; the Fairmont, St. Francis and Mark Hopkins, in San Francisco;

the Mayflower and Statler, in Washington; the Cleveland and Statler-Hilton, in Cleveland; the Kenilworth in Miami Beach; the Adolphus in Dallas; the Shamrock in Houston; the Deshler in Columbus; the Biltmore in Dayton; the Chase, Park Plaza and Statler-Hilton, in St. Louis; the Lord Baltimore in Baltimore; and the Chalfonte-Haddon Hall in Atlantic City.

Only the Sheraton hotels have forgotten me.

For there are invitations to share the hospitality also— and also on credit, at the Palacio and Del Prado, in Mexico City; the Caribe-Hilton in San Juan, Puerto Rico; El Panama in Panama City; the Castellana in Madrid; and the Istanbul-Hilton in Istanbul, Turkey.

How do I get there?

Well. Where I can drive, I now have a Hertz special charge card and a Greyhound rent-a-car card; together with a Phillips Petroleum Company executive courtesy card and a national credit identification card issued by Standard Oil Company (Indiana).

When I can't go by car, it is equally simple to go now, pay later. For I am the possessor of a TWA Ambassador Club card and an All Lines international air credit card!

For things to do with my time, I have become, in this same holiday mail, an accredited News Correspondent in radio and television with a Press Card entitling me to "all courtesies and privileges customarily accorded working newsmen," verified by *Broadcasting-Telecasting* Magazine. And, if it should be raining —I have been extended the courtesy of all of the studios of the National Broadcasting Company and the CBS and ABC radio and television networks, wherever.

In addition to the hotels that wish to be so kind to me in Chicago, I am assured that I am a member in good standing of a number of "clubs": Club Boyar, Club Andre, the Barclay, the Whitehall, the Chase, the Embers, the International Club in the Drake Hotel, and the Beau Nash in the Ambassador West.

For "meritorious service and staunch friendship" I have been commissioned a Grenadier of the House of Heileman, at La Crosse, Wis., by G. Heileman Brewing Company.

Finally, perhaps only to break the monotony of riotous living, I have been "appointed and commissioned an honorary deputy sheriff who is to equipt (sic) himself and hold himself in readiness to act officially at any time that he may be called on" by Robert E. Lee, Sheriff of Ware County, Georgia!

Fortunately, if I should accept even a few of these invitations, I am also declared a member of the Menninger Foundation of Topeka, Kansas: an institution for treatment and prevention in psychiatry.

1958

March 13

If you have wondered what a man does when he retires, you will find the list of Don Belding's current activities instructive.

Mr. Belding is chairman of the Freedoms Foundation at Valley Forge. He is national chairman of the 1958 Easter Seal Campaign for crippled children. He is a director of the American Heritage Foundation (and thus a client of our New York office, for the campaign to be run this Fall to elicit campaign funds for both parties from the rank and file of people).

On a local basis, but hardly less important, Don Belding is president of the Los Angeles Board of Airport Commissioners; vice-president of the Los Angeles Metropolitan Transit Authority and civilian aide to the Secretary of the Army for Southern California.

Mr. Belding is also a trustee and director of a number of other organizations, but these are his principal activities.

This is what retirement from advertising means.

April 23

I have had a great deal to say over the years about the Hallmark Hall of Fame and Mr. Hall's conviction that television can be a respectable and respected medium.

You will be pleased to read the opinion of the *New York Times* (Sunday, April 20) that "if all sponsors had Mr. Hall's respect for the integrity of the theatre and the intelligence of the American people, television would be a different and richer medium."

Sometimes I wonder if all too many advertisers do not fail to appreciate that integrity should bear a considerable amount of responsibility too.

*(I am of the opinion that it is the responsibility of adver-
tisers and broadcasters alike to maintain the integrity of television by supporting programs of special and even limited interest that are conceived and made with the highest order of
professionalism, not thrown together as a matter of conscience
—guilty conscience.*

*(That this can also pay off is illustrated by the success of
Hallmark's classic dramatic programs. Nor do I mean only
critical success. Hallmark cards are preferred by card buyers
in the ratio of 18 to 1 over the next best selling brand.)*

April 25

I hope you are reading James Thurber's reminiscences of
Harold Ross and *The New Yorker* in *The Atlantic Monthly*.
These began in the January issue.

Perhaps I want you to read them for a selfish reason. Ross
was hardly any more articulate about the material he wanted
in his magazine than Fred Ludekens and I sometimes are about
the things we want to see in our advertising. This causes me to
take heart.

If Ross could get out a consistently good magazine without
ever knowing exactly what it was he wanted until he saw it, and
in the blindness of the continuing rage against the forces of
apathy, I feel much better. So, I think, should you; because
while I may swear sometimes, I never throw things.

Anyway, all we want is what Harold Ross wanted and got.
And we want it in spite of our inability to always tell anyone
what it is.

Too much advertising today is crawling, creatively. Some
is even crawling backwards. Almost all of it is a copy of something else or a compromise between good advertising-making
and bad advertising direction.

And about all we want ours to be is important and clear
and quick to convince. Obviously, this is the hardest kind of
advertising to make. And the hardest to sell our clients; because
to make it we are always going to have to leave out things that
some of them want in.

June 24

Charles H. Brower, President of Batten, Barton, Durstine
& Osborn, recently made a talk at the National Sales Execu-

tives Convention in Washington, that pointed to something that should be of concern to all of us:

"The mediocrity of salesmanship (currently) is only a part of our national pattern of always being willing to settle for something less than the best. For this, in America, is the high tide of mediocrity, the great era of the goof-off, the age of the half-done job. The land from coast to coast has been enjoying a stampede away from responsibility. It is populated with laundry men who won't iron shirts, with waiters who won't serve, with carpenters who will come around someday maybe, with executives whose mind is on the golf course, with teachers who demand a single salary schedule so that achievement cannot be rewarded, nor poor work punished, with students who take cinch courses because the hard ones make them think, with spiritual delinquents of all kinds who have been triumphantly determined to enjoy what was known until the present crisis as 'the new leisure.' And the salesman who won't sell is only a part of this over-all mess.

"I think—and I hope to God it is true, that our people are becoming sick of this goofing off. The reason I do not know, but I will guess that we are gradually beginning to realize that history is repeating itself. The Russians are doing a wonderful job as the barbarians in our modern historical drama. But we are far outdoing them in our superlative imitation of Rome. We may lack a few of the refinements of Rome's final decadence but we do have the two-hour lunch, the three-day weekend and the all-day coffee break. And, if you want to, you can buy for $275, a jewelled pill box, with a built in musical alarm that reminds you (but not too harshly) that it's time to take your tranquilizer.

"Unquestionably, we are in a battle for survival. We must get our people into the battle. But first we have to get some battle into our people."

July 30

The new Chrysler advertising in newspapers and magazines clearly fails to answer the question as to whether any advertising people can shake the faith of the average automobile company executive in the everlasting cliches of the auto industry.

I don't believe there is a much better advertising agency in the business than Young & Rubicam and yet I read in Tuesday's *New York Times: "The mighty Chrysler makes driving exciting all over again"*; and then *"the excitement starts when your Chrysler dealer shows you that this Chrysler is as easy to own as it is to drive"*; finally there is the *"Mighty Chrysler . . . styled to excite . . . engineered to endure . . . priced to please"*.

All this around a wash drawing of a car with an amusement park roller coaster and simulated parachute jump gray in the background.

Here, it seems to me, is no excitement whatever; only words, words, words (including the standard alliteration. *"Now, big, brawny, beautiful Chryslers are priced right where you want them"*).

Thus Chrysler, like most of the other motor makers, plows deep into Detroit's advertising doldrums—where no real buyer problem is posed, no common experience explored, no answer to any want answered.

*

Unless they are considerably altered, the new Edsel advertisements will cut a quite different pattern.

(Alas, the planned advertising for the Edsel never got beyond the opening television spectacular. After the third successive management team got through with it, the last vestige of originality and low-key sincerity were out, and the standard Detroit bombast was in.

("An exciting new kind of car . . . styled to last. Engineered to last. And priced with the lowest priced three . . . gives you luxury without overdoing it.")

October 29

The following from a Wallachs advertisement (*New York Times,* October 27) registers a dissent with which I agree and which applies to most products as well as to the stores in which they are purchased.

It is entitled: THE AGE OF CHISELRY.

" . . . the age of the glorified discount and markdown . . . is in full bloom. It is not so much what you get but how much off that counts. Quality, service have

lost their meaning and value is lost in the bargain . . .
The biggest discount, however, is in the truth. Ficti-
tiously high prices are set so that a discount conscious
public can be enticed by imaginary savings . . .

Bulletin from Beacon Plastics

*

"When they first came along, discount houses, cut-rate
stores and the like were dismissed as a by-product of
the Great Depression. It was predicted that they could
never survive prosperity. But they did survive and
thrive.

"Today, most of the predictions run in the opposite direction. 'You can't beat the discounters.' 'People don't
want service anyway.' 'Pretty soon there won't be anything else *but* discount stores.'

"We dissent from both extremes. We think there will
always be discount houses of one kind or another.
There always has been and always will be someone
anxious to supply the buyer who puts price above
every other consideration. By the same token there
will always be customers who, in addition, have other
standards and who are repelled or attracted by the
very personality of a store."

Or, let me suggest again, the personality of a product.

December 8

It has been said by a good many substantial people that
when they know the facts of a story reported in *Time, Life* or
Fortune, that story is often colored or angled or just plain
wrong.

Certainly these magazines have been at pains to paint the
people of advertising as members of the lunatic fringe. They
almost never miss a chance for a snide description or a caustic
reference.

Now, *Fortune* (December) has attacked the whole television industry in an article that for sheer misrepresentation
probably has few equals on record. Television, says *Fortune,*
is fading out as an advertising medium.

An item which describes a total lack of impact for the Cros-
by-Sinatra spectacular for Edsel last Fall is typical. This could
easily have been corrected by the simple, normal expedient of

checking Ford's (and our) exhaustive research which showed
awareness of the new car and certain of its features to have
increased many times as the result of that broadcast! But
Fortune made no such check.

Goodness knows, television has its troubles and television
has had failures. But so have *Time, Life* and *Fortune.*

While TV network sales were up 10.6% during the first nine
months of 1958, *Life* had a 22.8% decrease in advertising lin-
age. *Time* was off 16.6%; *Fortune* was off 18%. And *Life* has
several times recently dropped its sale price to 19 cents (from
the standard quarter) to bolster vital newsstand sales in various
parts of the country.

I have known the publishers and advertising directors of
Time, Life and *Fortune* ever since any of these magazines began.
And I don't know any better people. But they have some strange
editorial associates.

And I hope that ABC, CBS and NBC will strike back hard
and publicly at *Fortune*—and *Time* and *Life,* too. They need to
be reminded of their obligation to be accurate.

(The editors of Fortune *had sounded the deathknell for
television and they weren't just about to take it back.)*

1959

February 10

This is about a number of different things ...

Journeying to the annual convention of the agency managers of the Equitable Life Assurance Society at Boca Raton, and
back, I discovered that the only real difference between the Central East Coast of Florida and Southern California, aside from
the fact that the latter lies in the shadow of high mountain
peaks, while Florida is flat as the top of my desk, is the wonderful green lushness of Florida's landscape. Southern California only matches this in rare small spots.

On the other hand, almost everything man-made is the
same—with a lack of originality that comes almost as a shock.

New clearings and new subdivisions are everywhere with
almost identical houses of cement block construction rising between and beside older clearings and older subdivisions with the
same almost identical houses, inevitably with jalousie windows

hooded like falcons in enveloping metal awnings that are probably the ugliest form of decoration yet developed for human
dwellings.

True, where Southern California has only ostrich farms,
Florida has alligator and monkey farms, and performing por-
poises, but the palm readers and curio shops and motels and
trailer courts offer the same threadbare promise of a good life
in the sun.

I'll still have to take Monterey with its crisp days and
nights. Or the invigorating airs of New England.

*

In Toronto, where the spick, span new office of Foote, Cone
& Belding is brightly efficient and where I had a first-rate dinner with the Olivers and Freemans at a French restaurant inexplicably called The Winston, I overheard an interesting dis-
sertation on commuting by train as a stimulation to reading.

Now, as a New York-Chicago commuter, I subscribe to this
reason for riding the planes only occasionally.

In two roundtrips between Chicago and New York, one via
Toronto, and in training to Florida and back, during January, I
managed to consume John O'Hara's *From the Terrace,* Peter
Drucker's *Landmarks of Tomorrow,* Romain Gary's *Roots of
Heaven,* and *Lady L,* Lederer and Burdick's *The Ugly American,*
Henry Slisar's *The Gray Flannel Shroud* (a mystery), Bernard
Dryer's *The Image Makers,* Nabokov's *Lolita,* Studdel's *The
Devil in Bucks County,* and certain chapters in *Agee on Film,*
and Robert Wood's *Suburbia.*

(Agee was probably the best serious critic the films have
ever had, and one of the best of recent American writers in any
case.)

*

The only trouble with the trains is almost everything.

Most of all on the trains of the New York Central System;
dilapidated, dirty and late. Robert R. Young once advertised,
"A hog can cross America without changing cars, but you
can't." This got the coast-to-coast Pullmans into operation.
Now Robert Young is dead. A suicide. The through Pullmans
are gone. Indeed, the Pullmans themselves have been removed
from the New York Central.

Nevertheless, the pig idea took root.

You can ride like one any day on the railroad that was

Young's. The effort to discourage passenger traffic may well become a model for getting rid of any unwanted obligation.

It is a shameful business, for readers and non-readers alike.

*

One more note.

I am a long-time admirer of Burnett Company advertising.

Just now, I particularly like their pages for Campbell's frozen soups. I love the headline, "A smoke house, a pea patch and patience" which it develops were prerequisite to the making of country-style split pea soup with ham. But I'll be damned if I didn't nearly throw up when I read about "coaxing the good flavors . . . until the very fragrance tempted every human within *sniffin'* distance."

The *makin's* for Marlboro scared me a little bit. But *sniffin'* makes it look like a frightening trend.

I am also bothered by a recent Santa Fe advertisement in *The New Yorker* which promises that in the ten-minute stop of the Super Chief at Albuquerque, New Mexico, "you'll meet full-blooded Pueblo Indians . . . fascinating people. Relive history."

All I can say is that if anybody can get even a grunt out of those moth-eaten, sad old Indians, let alone "relive history", I want to meet him.

But maybe whoever wrote that advertisement has never been on the station platform in Albuquerque for ten minutes.

February 18

The following by Sydney J. Harris in the *Chicago Daily News* of Monday, February 16, is something we can hope many people read:

> "The advertising profession has taken a terrible beating the last few years, in novels and films—because it is easy to dramatize and distort the high-powered activities of advertising agencies.

> "But in all fairness, I think that advertising has improved enormously in the last couple of decades—there are more better ads today than ever.

> "Moreover, the ad business has become increasingly critical of itself—perhaps more critical than any other profession. I read the journal, *Advertising Age,* every week, and its muscular candor about the faults of ad-

vertising are unrivaled by any other professional journal I know about.

"Neither the lawyers nor the doctors examine themselves with so skeptical and searching an eye as the ad people do. I have yet to see an editorial in the *AMA Journal* that suggested doctors were something less than guardian angels to the public; while the American Bar Association places lawyers only slightly lower than seraphim and cherubim.

"Even in my own profession, the leading trade paper, *Editor & Publisher,* is excessively sensitive to the feelings and prejudices of its readers. Criticism of the press, in its pages, is usually limited to a discreet murmur, even when there is plenty to shout about.

"The advertising people have taken a bum rap for years, and have often been blamed for the sins perpetrated by their clients. If the ordinary ad agency were given free rein, it would turn out ad copy that is tasteful, intelligent and appealing. The creative talent in the field is enormous.

"Even within the severe limitations imposed by short-sighted clients, I think the ad agencies have seen tremendous strides.

"If you compare the ads of today with those of a dozen years ago, you will find an immense superiority in today's artwork, copy and general attractiveness. There is more humor, more subtlety, more simplicity of a truly sophisticated sort.

"As a craftsman, I enjoy looking at ads, and I genuinely admire good ones. An ad that makes me feel the people behind it are warm and human, and not merely raucous barkers with a cash register for a heart, can motivate me to buy a product I would otherwise not have considered. This is a fact known to all ad agencies—but still by too few clients."

February 19

The use of humorous devices in television, particularly in animation, has proved valuable many times, either to emphasize points that are important about a product or to set the scene for straight selling.

The trouble with humor in printed advertising is that too often it fails of the advertising purpose.

A current advertisement for Bigelow carpet is a case in point. The full page in the *Saturday Evening Post* cartoons a man proposing to a girl, with the caption: "We won't need any furniture . . . we'll sleep on the Bigelow and eat at mother's." This, it seems to me, is only humor for the sake of fun. The caption neither makes a product point, nor leads to one.

On the other hand, humor used skillfully can be wonderfully attractive, as in this headline for a steamship advertisement in this week's *New Yorker:* "Purser Puckle Pampers Passengers—on Pacific & Orient Liners."

The thing is, there *is* a purser named Puckle. And you're delighted to meet him in the serious picture and story. The humor isn't dragged out.

February 24

The latest Green Giant corn advertisement has "corn-*lovin'* folks from Manhattan to Texas". And Kraft (who had a magnificent grape jelly ad in *Life* last week) also came up with "cheese for *pleasin'* someone special".

Maybe these things only bother *me*.

But then there are Mercury automobiles that now are "people-planned". And Vitasafe high-potency capsules that want to know if you are "suffering from TIRED LOVE?"

There is also the Cigar Institute of America that swears, "A cigar brings out the Matador in you."

Ole!

March 6

This is a follow-up on certain of the implications in Crawford Greenewalt's *The Uncommon Man.*

A terse article in *The Reader's Digest* for March shows how inflation has victimized everyone.

T. Coleman Andrews, former U. S. Commissioner of Internal Revenue, is the author, and his tables beat any argument that anyone has yet advanced upon the subject.

For example, to match the 1939 purchasing power of $3,000, it was necessary in 1957 to spend $7,370. A $10,000 income in 1939 took $30,971 to match it in 1957.

In 1939, the recipient of a $3,000 income had left after

taxes $2,943. In 1957, the same income after tax was worth only $1,265; income taxes had increased by $365 and inflation (reduced purchasing power) had taken away $1,313!

I am sending for reprints of the whole article, with tables for various incomes, and you will receive a copy.

March 10

I would be a lot more impressed with the final *Tide* Magazine panel report on television commercials whose top ten choices included Hallmark's Hall of Fame commercials as the only live entry, were it not for the fact that the panel's first choice for the second year in a row was the Bert and Harry series of animated spots for Piel's Beer in New York.

During the time these commercials have been on the air, constituting almost Piel's entire advertising effort, Piel Brothers, according to reliable figures, have dropped sharply in their share of New York beer sales!

*

There are some other advertising people who could be a little bit brighter too.

The setter that pointed so sharply and so handsomely in the advertisement in *Field and Stream* in September, 1958, as a result of eating Friskies, has now been discovered by Taylor Rhodes to have switched to Purina Dog Chow. At least this is what he is eating in *Field and Stream* this month.

The two advertisers used the identical photograph.

March 24

Almost ever since I can remember I have been reading maxims attributed to Gracian. Somewhere along the way I guess I had the idea, based on reading the Episcopal Hymn Book, that this was a counterpart of Anon.

It isn't.

Balthasar Gracian was a Spaniard who was born about 1600 in the Kingdom of Aragon, and died when he was Rector of the Jesuit College at Tarragona, in 1658. Three hundred and one years later, I have been presented with two copies (different translations) of his "Art of Worldly Wisdom," of which I never before had heard.

I commend these maxims to you, in the Joseph Jacobs' translation (the Macmillan Company, 1956) to read one at a time, perhaps one a day.

There is very little about people in this way-later age that Balthasar Gracian didn't contemplate three centuries ago, and lay out clearly and memorably.

April 7

I heard a fascinating talk one day last week on the program that Elwood Whitney arranged for the New York Art Directors Club on the subject of symbology.

The outstanding speaker was a Congregational missionary who has gone up and down the world for some thirty years bringing literacy to underdeveloped people.

The remarkable thing about this is that it is easy, as long as the symbols are clear and consistent. Illiterate Malayans can learn to read in two days. And how they want to! Reading means learning, and learning means food, and food is wealth.

How well the Chinese communists know this may be judged by the fact that the Chinese alphabet has been reduced from 285 often tortuous characters to only 20 Roman-like characters which are said to be the easiest in the world to learn to read. (There will be one billion literate Chinese within 20 years.)

English is the most difficult of all languages to learn to read because of the variations in vowel sounds, and the crazy spelling.

Example: GHOS could easily spell fish. GH as in laugh. O as in women. S as in sugar. Ghos, Fish!

June 11

I think the best of this year's new print advertising campaigns is the one for Kraft Jellies, made by Needham, Louis and Brorby. It is a great "picture" campaign rather than one made with a striking new theme or appeal. But here I think that, as Fred Ludekens has so often said, the words are *in* the picture.

The best outdoor posters that I have seen are (1) for the Bank of America in California (for the personal loan department), wherein a huge egg, breaking near the top, discloses two startled eyes, under the caption "Need More Room?", and (2) the current picture of a boy reclining in a porch chair eyeing a glass of Seven-Up as though it were nectar; the boy is out of Booth Tarkington rather than Mark Twain, and this is a happy development. The Seven-Up poster is from J. Walter Thompson

Company whose "Cars love Shell" posters will probably be the year's outstanding series.

(Lest anyone think I've gone soft on our competition, let me say that I think Thompson's testimonial campaign in magazines for the Portland Cement Association is almost classically formula-ridden. Why anyone should care what Bob Hope thinks about cement roads is beyond me. About golf balls, or even travelers cheques, yes. But not highways. For one thing, Hope always *flies* anything over a half-mile.)

Watch for the first of a new Kool-Aid series in *Life* for June 21.

And listen for the new Dash dog food radio commercials (particularly the one where the talking English bull dog addresses his master as "Guvnor").

July 10

One of the most shocking examples of the intelligent public's willingness to believe even the wildest libel of American business was the great success of Vance Packard's *The Hidden Persuaders*.

There was almost nothing implied in Mr. Packard's book about advertising that could not be refuted, and when I pointed this out in an article in *The Atlantic Monthly,* Packard himself could make no valid dissent.

Now Vance Packard has written another book, *The Status Seekers,* and it has headed the best-seller lists for non-fiction in both *The New York Times* and the *Chicago Tribune* for eight weeks.

I haven't read *The Status Seekers* and I don't intend to, for I know from experience that as Seymour M. Lipset makes clear in a review filled with corrections in *The Reporter,* for July 9, Mr. Packard purports to convey the findings of social science while misusing "scientific evidence to construct a prejudiced and partisan case".

His four principal theses are these: "That there has been a considerable (and haunting) growth in the American's concern with his social status; that there has been an (alarming) decline in social mobility, in the ability to move from one social class to another; that as a result of this decline the plight of the lower strata is actually worse 'subjectively' than it has ever been; and, finally, that there is a growing (and appalling) propensity for status-anxious Americans to become supercon-formists".

The parentheses are mine. But the ghosts are Mr. Pack-ard's; they are his chief stock in trade and he uses them in place of facts.

According to Mr. Lipset, the blurb on the jacket of *The Status Seekers* states as an accolade that the author is an associate member of the American Sociological Society.

And Mr. Lipset adds, "As one who sits on the membership committee of that Society, I would like to inform all intellectual status seekers that they too may become 'associate members' by paying twenty dollars, regardless of whether or not they ever took a course in sociology, or for that matter whether they ever went to college. The manner of the blurb is consistent with the matter of this book".

Vance Packard reminds me of a rocking chair adventurer Fred Ludekens and I once knew who had printed on his letter-head, "Member, National Geographic Society", which is what everyone becomes when he subscribes to *The National Geographic Magazine.*

September 22

We hear so often that there is no difference between brands and the choice is only something cooked up by advertising that I think you will be interested in the following from the latest issue of *The Public Pulse,* published on occasion by Elmo Roper and Associates:

"Product differentiation may have diminished over the years, but it has not entirely disappeared. This was demonstrated clearly, although somewhat inadvertently, in a recent test of two brands of cigarettes.

"For test purposes, the two brands were stripped of identifying labels and put in plain white packages, differentiated only by neutral symbols. Respondents were asked to smoke one pack of each brand and report preferences.

"The results were curious: although among the sample *as a whole,* the preferences were very close, *habitual smokers* of Brand X showed a definite preference for Brand Y—and vice versa. An examination of reasons showed no erratic deviation from character on the part of smokers: Brand X smokers said they liked Brand Y for qualities usually ascribed to Brand X—

and again vice versa. A scrupulous check of statistical tabulations showed no slip-up there.

"When finally the puzzling predicament was presented—with some embarrassment—to the client, he was able to hunt down the answer: when the cigarettes were packed the sample lots had been accidentally switched. Thus the statistics on Brand Y really applied to Brand X, turning the findings downside up.

"Moral of the piece: Most cigarette smokers *do* know their own brands. If they did not, the test results would have been meaningless rather than puzzling, and the switch in packing would have gone unnoticed."

October 12

You never know what kind of assignments you are going to get in this business.

Recently our client, the Southern Pacific Company, asked our people in San Francisco to design and supervise the printing of several bilingual pieces—breakfast and luncheon menus and beverage list—for Mr. Khrushchev and his party aboard a special Southern Pacific train carrying them from Los Angeles to San Francisco.

Bill Matthews reports that the job had to be completed in five days. Since we have no writers of Russian in our Copy Department and no experts in foreign protocol, this was no simple exercise for our Southern Pacific group.

There were almost as many considerations involved as in the preparation of the most serious marketing or media plans. And it was only with the help of the U. S. State Department and the Berlitz School of Languages and the Russian interpreter for the Mayor of San Francisco and numerous other individuals and organizations, including a patient printer, that our people were able to get the job done on time.

The result, however, was excellent. The Russians were not only able to read their Southern Pacific menus, but they could also order the food they wanted in a way the dining car waiters could understand, for the Russian and English equivalents were printed side by side and the Russians had only to check the ones they wanted.

October 13

I think it might not be a bad idea if the people who write

our advertising and illustrate it and research it and present it to our clients would read in last week's *Advertising Age* a talk I made two months ago at Sidney Bernstein's and Steuart Britt's annual advertising workshop.

Perhaps this will explain and illustrate what I believe all good advertising should be and do. That this piece is devoted to printed advertising (which I think is much the hardest kind to make) has nothing to do with certain rules for all advertising. The fact that many of these are broken daily by television commercials proves only that bad advertising can succeed with captive audiences. It doesn't make the rules any different because it doesn't tell what good commercials might do in the place of the very bad ones.

The reason for this memo today is twofold. One is an article that I read over the weekend about the current success of an advertising agency that has yet to produce an original idea that I know of. It has simply adopted someone else's bold advertising techniques to several of its own jobs. There isn't a sensible selling idea in it.

The second reason for this memo is the sickness I feel about the business we are in when I contemplate the introductory advertising of the "all-new" 1960 automobiles.

For the most part, this is either made cynically to draw boobs into salesrooms to buy new fractional advantages and totally unimportant changes, or simply to please certain manufacturers who have never been pleased by anything yet unless it was almost precisely what everyone else in the industry was doing.

Even the advertising of the new compact cars is mincing and unconvincing as if most of the manufacturers were not sure at all whether they really want to sell these.

The campaign that we have proposed for Lincoln and Continental next year, happily, is no copy of anything. And it makes no compromises.

Nor do many of our others.

But read the piece in *Advertising Age* that restates, and illustrates as well as I can with exhibits from other advertising agencies, the philosophy that I believe in.

December 22

This is the time of year when almost everyone is making

some kind of prediction about the months ahead. The beginning of a new decade, with cold war and hot peace, and the newest flights of science into the unknown, have taken the wraps off imagination everywhere.

Amidst the outlook from the laboratories and toward the summit, and the disappearance of the individual from the world below, the current breast beating in advertising is hardly of great significance.

Nevertheless there are a number of us in this business who are troubled by the bad things in it, and while it is doubtful that anything much will be done about these with lasting effect in the nineteen-sixties, I do think that personal dignity demands of some of us that we try to do something.

As a result of the eruption in television, the general organizations of advertising have become sensitive and self-conscious. The American Association of Advertising Agencies, for instance, has revived its Interchange, which is a receiving center for professional complaints about members' transgressions. But it is perhaps significant that no one has ever been kicked out of the Association for cutting capers.

The Association of National Advertisers, which also treats the horns of large bulls very gently, is reported to be edging into the fracas with a program to explain the function and value of advertising!

And the Advertising Federation of America, which is a kind of national league of local advertising clubs, holds to the rather quaint notion that most of the trouble with advertising stems from a lack of widespread understanding and appreciation of its virtues and wants it to be loved by everyone. Soon the A.F.A. will move its headquarters from New York to Washington to be nearer the suspicious Congress.

To suggest that much of this activity is unpromising under present circumstances is only to repeat what I have said before.

The organizations of advertising will have to do better.

The problem of dishonest and distasteful advertising is not going to be solved either by gentle pressure from the side of the angels or the slow processes of education; and to try to ignore it as a small percentage of all advertising is to be insensitive to right and wrong.

It is here. It is real. And, whatever the percentage, the amount of bad advertising is large and it is not diminishing. The only unknown is why the people who could kill it let it live.

Newspapers, magazines, television and radio could clean up advertising with their next closing dates by the simple expedient of demanding proof of claims (How can four different cigarettes all be lowest in nicotine, lowest in tars; how can three different headache remedies all work fastest?). Many leading newspapers and magazines already demand such proof, and all the other reputable publishers and all the broadcasters could, too.

The cause of truth in advertising already has all the organizations it needs in the Federal Trade Commission, the Federal Drug Administration, the Federal Communications Commission, the Post Office Department and the Better Business Bureaus. It only requires the cooperation of the media of advertising to insist that none of these bodies shall be thwarted by the continued acceptance by the media of unproved claims and tasteless promises.

The Advertising Federation's opposition to anti-advertising measures in legislation is probably sound, for most of these tend to be discriminatory. However, the A.F.A. traditionally behaves toward advertising like cucumber growers during National Pickle Week, and it is to be hoped that its approach to some of the legislative problems of advertising will be on a considerably more thoughtful plane.

As for the A.N.A., it could save a lot of time and money because the function of advertising is already known: it is to be there when you can't go in person; to present your proposition in your absence. How it should appear and what it should promise are the questions to be answered; and I hope the A.N.A. will address itself to these.

The importance of advertising is perfectly clear. And the A.N.A. and the 4A's and the A.F.A. will do well to support the good people in it and loudly and fearlessly condemn the bad ones and stop worrying about advertising as an institution.

Dishonest and ugly advertising is going to be with us just so long as there are dishonest and ugly advertisers and hungry media people and unscrupulous advertising agents. The only change next year or in the next ten years will be brought about by those advertisers and media owners and agency people whose principal concern with the fast buck ceases to be unconcern.

Foote, Cone & Belding and its clients, and most other agencies and their clients, are honest. The thing we have to watch for is the exception, and whenever we find one we should refuse to appear in his company, either in print or on the air. This is the way we can help those media that just may, sometimes, be unable to make up their own minds.

What makes this all a matter of some importance is the odds-on probability that advertising in the decade ahead will increase at least in ratio to the population, and it must not be used cynically.

(No advertiser ever hesitates to scream about a poorly printed page in a magazine or a messed up commercial in television. And I don't see why they shouldn't object equally to a polluted advertising atmosphere.

(Several years ago I reacted strenuously to a salacious advertisement in Collier's *by Elliott White Springs, a World War I aviator, for his Springs Mills bed sheets, and told the publisher that if* Collier's *carried any more of Springs' suggestive copy I was going to recommend to our clients that they drop the magazine from their media lists. I simply didn't want any of our clients' advertising contaminated by Mr. Springs' tastelessness.*

(I received an outraged letter from Springs. But his advertising never appeared in Collier's *again.)*

1960

January 7

Ernie Eversz clipped the following from *Advertising Age* for January 4.

It was written by David Ogilvy in a year-end message to his staff, and I couldn't agree more heartily with his point of view.

"I hope you will be happy here. The qualities which we most admire, and which are most likely to bring you promotion, are these:

"1. First, we admire people who *work hard*. We dislike passengers who don't pull their weight in the boat.

"2. We admire people with first-class brains, because you cannot run a great advertising agency without brainy people.

"3. We admire people who *avoid office politics*.

"4. We despise toadies who suck up to their bosses;

they are generally the same people who bully their subordinates.

"5. We admire the great professionals, the craftsmen who do their jobs with superlative excellence. These people always respect the professional expertise of their colleagues in other departments.

"6. We admire people who hire subordinates who are good enough to succeed them. We pity people who are so insecure that they feel compelled to hire inferior specimens as their subordinates.

"7. We admire people who build up and develop their subordinates, because this is the only way we can promote from within the ranks. We detest having to go outside to fill important jobs.

"8. We admire people who practice delegation. The more you delegate, the more responsibility will be loaded upon you.

"9. We admire kindly people with gentle manners who treat other people as human beings—particularly the people who sell things to us. We abhor *quarrelsome* people. We abhor people who wage paper warfare. We abhor buckpassers, and people who don't tell the truth.

"10. We admire well-organized people who keep their offices shipshape, and deliver their work on time.

"11. We admire people who are good citizens in their communities — people who work for their local hospital, their church, the PTA, the Community Chest and so on."

I would hope that we could be admired on all counts.

March 9

Recently I made a talk in Los Angeles about the general situation in television. This was commented upon rather widely in the press and there was considerable agreement on two points. These are excerpted in the following:

"Most of the agitation today for different programming is based on a conviction that persists that our programs are somehow the result of advertising's hold on television; and that this hold must now be broken.

"This is *our* dilemma: the advertisers and their agents, and the networks and stations. For the truth is that there is no advertising hold. What there is, is a clear-cut preference by the majority of television viewers for regular programs of the type that make up the top of the Nielsen list. And advertisers buy these to talk to everyone they can; just as they buy space in *The Reader's Digest* and *Life* and *Look* and *The Saturday Evening Post* and the Sunday supplements for the largest circulations available.

"The difference is that the supplements and *The Saturday Evening Post* and *Look* and *Life* and *The Reader's Digest* sell advertising space on the basis of their total circulation for all the varied things magazines contain; just as do the newspapers; while television is bought, or sold, for special segments of its total weekly broadcast.

"The problem thus becomes: how to include in this total the kind of broad fare the magazines and newspapers provide when the television audience is vastly different for different kinds of programs; and how to get this total paid for.

"One advertiser, it seems to me, can hardly be expected to pay two or three or four times as much per thousand viewers, as another.

"However, I think there is a way out.

"Forgetting what I believe to be the unreasonable prejudice that exists against the advertiser as an unholy patron of television (while he is a benign one of the press), I think the critics are rightly dismayed by the plight of the minority of viewers whose desire for more intellectual stimulation and satisfaction from television is fulfilled all too rarely. Or under painful circumstances.

"If one chooses, for example, to watch *Our American Heritage,* or a discussion of the U. S. in world affairs, or something like the *Margaret Bourke-White Story,* a story of triumph over disease, then one must forego *Ed Sullivan,* or *Maverick* or *Lawman.* Whatever program one chooses to view eliminates all simultaneous programs forever.

"This last condition won't be changed until we all have automatic, built-in tape recorders; and libraries for film; and players to play the film. This is not yet. And even when we do have these things, *Wagon Train* and *Perry Mason* and *Leave it to Beaver* are going to have more viewers than *Meet the Press* or *Small World* at any hour when there is a choice.

"Meanwhile, the problem remains; for the fact remains also that it is everybody's air that the broadcasters and the advertisers are using; and if, as I believe, they are satisfying a large majority in their use of this air today, there is another group, a minority, that has some rights tomorrow.

"Unfortunately, in my opinion, this latter group, this minority—like almost all minorities, has been overlooked, or overridden, until its cause has become an intellectual and political cause through our neglect together. Television has been a business to make money in. And not, primarily, a way to serve.

"This is wrong.

"Exactly how broadcasting, and advertising, will answer their critics, and particularly their sincere critics, of whom there are many, I can't be sure. The scheduling of an hour each week, by each network, of what is called 'informational, cultural and educational programs', with a half-hour every third week for local programs in these same interests, may be a beginning. I hope it is. But I deplore the fact that even this beginning, if it is one, came out of what seems to be an agreement with the Federal Communications Commission—to trade-up television by decree.

"Let us decry the notion that any Committee or Commission is any more necessary to responsible television broadcasting than to the responsible theatre or the movies or the press.

"I know there are differences in these various means of communication. But I can't believe there is any difference at all in the accountability that each one has to itself and to its audience, to the public it serves, to be free. If I am right, then the responsibility for programming is the networks' and the stations'. And they must be responsible to the public as a whole; with all the forces of advertising on the side of encouragement.

"One way that television could program for all the public, and still deal fairly with the advertisers who must pay the freight, would be according to the British system of the English ABC where advertisers' announcements are rotated, between programs, through the network's own planned schedule.

"This has been called the 'magazine concept'. And there are a good many people who think that we will come to it eventually.

"Certainly this 'magazine concept' for television has the virtue of putting the responsibility for programming precisely where most people think it belongs. However, it must be remembered that America's advertisers have so far borne *all* the costs of television; they are senior partners in the enterprise; and, as such, they are not lightly to be denied any choice in the programs they pay for.

"But maybe there is another way to bring about the broader programming that is desirable, still with joint program responsibility. What we are after is to continue to please the majority that wants mostly entertainment, while adding more cultural, or intellectual, programs for the minority—and to trade-up all programming. And I think there is a way. In fact, I think there are two ways. Or two *parts* to this thing.

"The first seems to me fairly simple, and only slightly more costly for the networks and stations.

"At present most evening network programs are sold to the advertisers on an alternate-week basis. This means that they purchase 26 programs. However, these programs are subject to two preemptions, which cuts down the advertiser's participation to 24 (plus his alternate weekly spots) — and makes way for such special programs as the Hallmark *Hall of Fame, Playhouse 90, Sunday Showcase* and the spectaculars.

"Well, I suggest merely that four of each 24 programs be rescheduled with other than the regular features. For instance, if the advertiser's regular program feature is *Have Gun,* or *Danny Thomas* or *Red Skelton,* he would have twenty of these, scheduled five-in-a-row, with every sixth program devoted to political discussion, scientific developments, adventures in the arts, or whatever might be developed for intellectual viewing.

"This would place not an hour a week on each of the three networks in the service of information, education and culture, but an hour and a half each night; or more when there are hour programs on a network.

"I have an idea that this would be acceptable to a good many advertisers if only the price for the programs of narrower interest were made commensurate with the audiences delivered. Actually, the only question I see here is whether the networks and the stations will willingly decrease their take.

"So far they have been *unwilling* to do this. Advertisers pay the same amount for time for a 15-rating show that they pay for a 30-rating program. And this you know is going to change. If it does so in connection with re-programming, then I think everyone is going to gain from the changes.

"The second part of this proposal, which was given to me by Jack Simpson, who is director of all the broadcasting activities in Foote, Cone & Belding, strikes at *two* things.

"First of all, it gets at the matter of rigidity in the television medium that makes it impossible to view two different programs that are broadcast at the same time. Second, Mr. Simpson's proposal, or the one he expressed to me, offers relief for the first time to an industry that is using up creative talent much faster than it can be recruited; a fact that has more than a little to do with the present level of broadcasting.

"Again, this is a very simple proposal: for it is only to take all this week's programs, save the news, and play them again next week; to repeat each program except the news and weather programs, a second time, in the same time period on the same day, once. Thus, instead of every program viewed eliminating two other programs where the time is the same, there would be an opportunity to view *two* out of every *three* programs broadcast. That these could be a much better two out of a much better three follows from the reduction of some 3,000 hours of annual nighttime network programming to 1,500 hours.

"Surely, this could be tested easily, anywhere, at any time.

"At any rate, I offer both these suggestions seriously."

*

So far neither Mr. Stanton nor Mr. Sarnoff nor Mr. Goldenson has taken notice.

(Despite the unenthusiasm of the networks, and perhaps more to the point, the stations, there have occurred two distinct developments that bring my suggestions closer to fulfillment.

(Most advertisers today buy participations in a number of programs, rather than programs as a whole. Also, almost all the programs in the first half of the television season [October through March] are repeated in the second half [April through September].

(Under the circumstances, there is no reason why advertisers shouldn't participate in total programming. Or why programs of entertainment or information [other than news] shouldn't be repeated a week after the initial broadcast.

(Having come half way, I think the time is ripe to take the final steps.)

August 29

Time's review of John Gunther's story of Albert D. Lasker, in the current issue, appears beneath the scurvy caption: Prince of Hucksters.

Huckster is one of *Time's* most contemptuous terms. And *Time,* by omission, makes it stand up. For example: "When a Quaker Oats' product, Wheat Berries, got nowhere, Lasker changed the name to Puffed Wheat, 'the grains that are shot from guns,' and business ballooned." The implication is that this was hanky-panky.

But was it?

What *Time* doesn't tell (although Gunther does) is that when Claude Hopkins, Lord & Thomas' famous copywriter, visited a Quaker Oats plant, "something that was being taken altogether for granted caught his alert, artful eye. He saw a mechanism, an instrument like a drum or blunt cannon, in which the grains were subjected to pressure; then they were exploded upward, puffed out to eight times their normal size."

These became Puffed Wheat and Puffed Rice, "the grains that are shot from guns." And I can only wonder what chicanery there was here, or elsewhere in the story of Albert Lasker, except in some *Time* writer's jaundiced eye.

That there are hucksters in advertising, nobody can deny. There always have been; just as there have always been quacks in medicine and shysters at the bar. But Albert Lasker was not one of them.

October 3

The Waste Makers by Vance Packard is the second rehash of the same wild accusations of corruption in business, and particularly marketing, that he first unleashed in *The Hidden Persuaders* and rewrote in *The Status Seekers.*

Much closer than any evidence he supplies in his book to prove the excessive power of advertising and the gullibility of the public is the wide sale of Packard's heavily-advertised books.

Incidentally, I was amazed to read an unquestioning review of *The Waste Makers* in yesterday's *Sun-Times,* and a line in the *Tribune* review that called Packard "an extremely competent reporter of the social scene."

Since he presents only one side of any argument that he constructs, he gives his readers no hint at all that there is another side. Actually, Vance Packard uses facts solely to distort them; the rest of the time he builds his own accusations of conspicuous waste into highly charged generalizations for which the only basis is his word.

Gold-plated toothbrushes, which he says are "soaring" in popularity, is a fair example. How many people, I wonder, have even heard of these things?

Mr. Packard is a dishonest writer. And David McKay Co., his publisher, is a dishonest publisher, for all of the inaccuracies and all the fallacies that were pointed out in the first of the Packard books here are repeated again and enlarged.

October 10

For as long as I can remember I have stood up for the press against every accusation that it is corruptible by advertising.

I am sure that it is not; just as I am sure that neither advertisers nor advertising people have any wish to corrupt it. For good selfish reasons all want the press strong.

However, I think there is a growing section of the press that is being corrupted from within. For much as television suffers from a shortage of talent, so do the magazines; and the result is sloppy reporting, much too little checking of facts and a growing tendency to slant stories to make them sensational.

There is no question but what *Time* has been doing this for years. And now we have in the current *Saturday Evening Post,* in an article on Chicago by John Bartlow Martin, an example of another kind of corrupt journalism. This is from the Vance Packard school which consists of telling one side of a story in such a way as to say, without coming right out with it, that there is no other side.

Mr. Martin rehashes Chicago's crime problems from Capone to the burglar Morrison with an airy disposal of almost everything else about the city that he says is "quite possibly the worst city to live in in the United States." New York is Martin's other possibility.

Typical of this kind of editorial malignancy is an illustration of a sordid back alley in what is called Chicago's "south side jungle of poverty and crime." But there is no picture, nor even a word about the new Lake Meadows and Prairie Shores redevelopment projects that were made to cut down the jungle. An instance of the new technique of making a statement into a fact by implying wide application of it is in the suggestion that "crime is Chicago's favorite sport." According to Martin, a visitor (discussing crime) said to him recently, "This is your baseball."

I recommend Mr. Martin's piece to our agency students of media to see how low journalism can sink. Television is almost noble by comparison.

October 17

It would be much easier to argue with some of the critics of all advertising if certain specific advertising didn't lend itself to very proper criticism.

A case in point was the General Motors commercials in the World Series broadcasts. These obviously were made for people who credit the public with very little intelligence and no taste whatever.

The animation recalled the first days of television, the comedy was Katzenjammer and the music hardly more distinguished than Michigan Avenue's little old lady with the hand organ.

I think I have heard more talk about these commercials than about any others in months, and it was all bad.

Gillette, Toni and Paper-Mate built a high standard for the Series over a period of years.

Then General Motors knocked it down in a week.

This is one of those cases where it is hard to believe that an advertising agency could have been responsible. But then, this is the case almost all through automobile advertising.

(General Motors Chevrolet division has since aired some of the most imaginative and beautifully produced commercials yet to appear on television.

(Cars moving without drivers through night-lit Paris streets have not been topped by anyone.)

November 15

One of the most remarkable developments in the annals of the advertising business was reported last week in *Printers' Ink*.

Jack Tinker, creative head at McCann-Erickson; Herta Herzog and two other McCannics have been set up in an apartment in New York's midtown Dorset Hotel, removed from the rustle and bustle of the agency, simply to create!

No assignments. No deadlines. Presumably no clients. Just the contemplation of new ideas and new concepts.

Like Einstein.

November 17

Perhaps I shouldn't look so wryly at McCann's pure creative group—the one that is reported to be without assignment other than to think. After all, Marion Harper has a lot better record for building a large agency than I have.

Besides, the total non-creative (or, may I say, non-sensical) output of some of our highly regarded advertising agencies today is almost appalling. The dedication of several of them to a thing called impact, which has nothing to do with the impact of ideas but only with over-size pictures of products without physical differences, and large type in wide measure to cover up the absence of any argument, is making a good deal of printed advertising look pretty silly.

Television advertising is only a little bit better, because it is easier to make. So maybe McCann has something. Maybe they'll even discover that advertising is only a substitute for calling on someone, and that it should be based primarily on what you would say to that someone if you *could* call.

November 30

For several years I have been reading about awards to the makers of amusing animated television commercials for Piel's Beer in New York. According to any number of studies, Bert and Harry (Piel) were the favorite advertising characters of the TV audience and the critics alike; they were off-beat.

Somehow, I could never believe that Bert and Harry were selling beer. Still they stayed on the air: "fresh, amusing, adult" and, I repeat, off-beat. That is, they stayed on the air until last week. Now they are gone.

Piel's Beer has actually shown a *loss* in share of the New York market during their incumbency.

December 28

In looking at advertising and its media during 1960, and peering into 1961, I must admit there are certain areas that seem to defy either time or talent to improve them very much.

Perhaps this is true in advertising mostly because so many

of the products involved lack any but obvious differences on the one hand and only differences that one may put into them subjectively, on the other. Automobiles are in the first category; their differences are largely in the size and power and luxury the various prices cover. The result is that within each price group the battle of superlatives creates a din in which a single voice is rarely heard and almost no advertising stands out.

Volkswagen is the only continuing exception.

It just may be that advertising has very little to do with auto sales anyway; only making each year's new models recognizable before the public begins to see them on the street. This, incidentally, is no small feat—what with the copying, line for line. The automobile makers invariably adopt the worst of their competitors' features; they are like the movie producers who currently are exhibiting half a dozen films whose heroines are sweet-hearted prostitutes.

Subjective product differences lead to the advertisers' greatest offenses. Or maybe this is just the silly side of advertising, and people.

In any case, in a recent single issue of the *New Yorker* one might have wondered how Coty's L'Or could be the world's most luxurious perfume while Patou's Joy is the costliest, or how Lanvin's My Sin is the best Paris has to offer at the same time that Monteil's Nostalgia is the most luxurious of *all* French perfumes. Jolie Madame, by Balmain, is called the most sophisticated, but Corday's Trapeze has danger in every drop, and D'Orsay's VoulezVous is the spark that starts the fire!

The *New Yorker,* it would appear, is not only pretty sophisticated about advertising ("There'll always be an Adman"), but also pretty indulgent, at a healthy page rate.

However, the *New Yorker's* careful two-part story of the failure of the Edsel, by John Brooks, gave a straight answer to a point that is argued at length in the writings of Vance Packard, J. K. Galbraith, Arthur Schlesinger, Jr., etc., who hold that the public is subject to endless, evil manipulation by advertisers. The fact is, and nothing proves it better than the unhappy story of the Edsel, that the public makes its own decisions and it makes them on its own personal appraisals of what is offered.

Advertising may make people look, and frequently it does, but it can't make them accept anything; this is up to the product or the service that is advertised, and what truthfully and convincingly can be said about it.

In just this way, household products advertising, which makes up the largest if not the noisiest industry classification, and by far the largest classification in Foote, Cone & Belding, continues to become more useful and more appealing. Better copy, plainer copy that is, better art, better photography and, above all, better reproduction, are helping to brighten magazine and newspaper pages considerably.

The threat of Federal Trade Commission action, under the forthright direction of Earl W. Kintner, has had a salutary effect upon most of the confirmed chiselers, and television advertising as a whole is becoming more restrained if not more artistic.

The trouble is, television advertising, being much more intrusive than printed advertising and thus more quickly worn out, burns up advertising talents just as television entertainment burns up the talents of writers, directors and performers. The search is for more and more off-beat and tricky approaches that will somehow relieve the tedium. The idea is to make entertainment out of advertising for entertainment's sake, and this kind of tax upon advertising may well be too great. At any rate, the test is on.

In the pure entertainment field of television programming, the only test is of how much the public can stand of the very same stuff: how many Westerns, how many private eyes, how many guessing games, how many situation comedies?

Possibilities announced for the Fall of 1961 include a Canadian version of I Remember Mama, a biblical Wagon Train, a situation comedy which is described as another Father Knows Best; Li'l Abner following Dennis the Menace over from the comics, a series built around an eccentric professor who can be expected to be a masculine Eve Arden, a haunted house anthology, another series of big city crime stories which is likened to Naked City, Bachelor Girl—which will presumably be a female version of Bachelor Father. George Gobel will be offered again, this time as a free-lance writer. Mickey Rooney will be a small town publisher. Brian Gallagher will be a syndicated newspaper columnist. Jan Clayton will operate a restaurant, much as Ann Sothern operates a hotel. Hugga Mugga will be an "adult" cartoon program taking its cue from The Flintstones.

And so, on and on.

Nevertheless, the television people have been listening to their critics. Special programs like this year's magnificent Macbeth and the ambitious Golden Child on Hallmark's Hall of Fame, An Evening with Fred Astaire, and some of the Shirley Temple shows will continue to be exceptions. The great difficulty here is obvious: original entertainment is hard to come by. When it takes so long to produce and when it is exhausted so quickly in television, it is almost certain to be made for the stage and the screen first. Not so, however, the documentary. This, it is clear from this year's beginnings, from the CBS Reports and the other increasingly thoughtful and often highly controversial and lively documentaries on all sorts of subjects on all three networks, affords television a unique opportunity, and the networks and the stations are aiming to make the most of it.

In Chicago, WGN-TV, under the direction of Ward Quaal, has emerged as a fourth important source of programming, particularly in its news coverage.

Altogether, television is settling into a new pattern. And if there is a good deal of it that lacks imagination, this is the pattern also of magazine content and the movies; and if one remembers that the *Atlantic* and *Harpers* appear only once a month, the *New Yorker* and the *Saturday Review* only weekly, and the *Reporter* only every other week, I suspect that Sunday on television, and the scattering of intellectually stimulating programs among the week night hours, will measure up fairly well to the standards of our other mass media of communications which, taken together, and including the general and news weeklies, probably are the highest they have ever been.

I know that it is fashionable to complain, and I am not content. But I think a great many people in broadcasting, publishing and advertising alike, are trying to do their best. The question, of course, will always be "what is best?" and "who says so?" The only suggestion that seems to make sense is to choose your friends and never mind the rest.

1961

January 23

Perhaps I shouldn't worry about critics of our business when it is obvious that they know nothing about it.

Nevertheless, I was dumbfounded when I read in a review of John Gunther's book in *The Economist* (London, December 31) that when Albert Lasker retired from advertising in 1942 he *"turned over a completely new leaf."*

To be sure, Mr. Lasker devoted his life after his retirement to art, medical research and health insurance, and to a long list of other items in the public interest. However, there was nothing new to him in public service. He had headed the U. S. Shipping Board. He had put in Judge Landis to clean up baseball. He was instrumental in the appointment of a former cabinet member, Will Hays, to police the wayward moving picture industry. Also he was an active trustee of the University of Chicago during much of the exciting and controversial administration of Robert Maynard Hutchins as Chancellor. And he did all these things while he was head of the advertising agency of Lord & Thomas.

Afterwards, I saw Mr. Lasker hundreds of times in New York, where he lived; if he ever came to Chicago without writing me or, at least, telephoning, I am not aware of this; and what we talked about mostly was *advertising*. Among other things Mr. Lasker didn't think that Foote, Cone & Belding was making nearly as much money as he thought we should.

There were many things *in* advertising that Albert Lasker decried, but advertising itself was not one of them.

March 10

I think we are pretty consistent in our philosophy, which is to make advertising that is clear and rewarding to anyone who comes within sight or sound of it.

But I think we fail more often than we should to get the best possible illustrations for the things that we are trying to make clear. This applies equally to print and television. We sometimes seem willing to choose between alternatives when each leaves something to be desired. And this is not good.

It is our job to see to it not only that what we are trying to illustrate is illustratable, but also that the illustrations themselves follow the rules for good advertising.

There should be no compromises.

I would like to see us reject more photographs and more film. We tear up a good many headlines and a great deal of copy in the course of a month, simply because we think we can do better; and I see no reason why the people we pay to implement our words in pictures, either still or moving, or made with camera, brush or pen, shouldn't be asked to do likewise.

The level of advertising just now is not very high. Some longtime very good agencies appear to be floundering around, uncertainly. It is almost as if they can't make up their minds between the "hard sell" and the "soft sell", and in between these, the "cute sell".

I think we know well enough that only the *sensible sell* is worth putting into print or onto television. But I also think we must put it there superlatively well. The total weight of today's advertising can't be penetrated any other way.

March 14

There were several interesting items in *Printers' Ink* last week (March 10).

One tells how the enterprising people at J. Walter Thompson Company "conceived the idea that 'Peanuts' characters could be perfect representatives of all Ford sought to convey for its Falcon. A happy coincidence for all parties was the fact that Schultz (the artist) was a long-time and satisfied Ford user. His preference for the automobile made him consent all the more readily to commercial use of his characters."

What makes this interesting is that the Thompson people conceived the idea of using the "Peanuts" characters only after they had been introduced into advertising by Foote, Cone & Belding via posters for The First National Bank of Chicago, where they cavorted for almost a year. In our case it was Mr. Schultz's devotion to money (and I don't mean the bank's $3 billion in deposits) that made him consent to the commercial use of his characters.

When Thompson and Ford offered him more of the green stuff he switched. I don't know that I blame him; cartoonists have to make it while they can. But I hate to read that the reason was love; and that the Thompson company discovered "Peanuts," as it were.

The second item of special interest explains how Purex, through Edward H. Weiss; Bell & Howell, through McCann; Chuck Ryan at Firestone; Dick Pinkham at Bates, and Leo Burnett, for Philip Morris, have made the startling discovery that selective audiences in television may do very well indeed; that great masses of viewers are not always necessary to advertising success.

This I find interesting because the discovery heralded here was made by Mr. Joyce C. Hall, of Hallmark Cards, in the infancy of television, and everyone in Foote, Cone & Belding has known it ever since. Witness: "Our American Heritage" for the Equitable, which also is the subject of an enthusiastic article in the same issue of *Printers' Ink.*

(How things change!

(When I came into the advertising business in 1926, Printers' Ink *was its bible—a* Reader's Digest *size magazine that reprinted innumerable speeches spiced with bits of news, in a rich garden of advertising.*

(Then came Advertising Age, *a real news magazine with an able reporting staff, and* Printers' Ink, Advertising & Selling, Tide [Time's *entry into the field] and* The Advertiser, *all bit the dust.)*

March 16

There is a single line in each of the advertisements in the *Chicago Tribune's* current campaign in behalf of business that says something to remember.

Offer a good value at a good price and customers will respond, is what it says, and I think this is a good deal better advice than is usually given by people in the advertising business. It is certainly vital to "have faith in a growing America" as has been suggested recently at each recession. But to urge people to prove their faith by spending money simply to make the wheels of industry turn faster seems to me to be a frightful proposition.

This is the kind of sophistry that keeps scornful books like *The Affluent Society* and *The Waste Makers* high in the best-seller lists for months as it gives the public tangible evidence upon which to share their authors' concern about industry's selfish purpose and the immoral role of advertising in support of this.

Good values at good prices probably offers more hope for stemming the present recession than anything else that will be proposed. I have an idea that poor values at high prices in a number of industries has had more than a little to do with our troubles. The American public is not simple-minded. It falls for some pretty incredible propositions (like longer, longer, lower, lower, costlier and costlier automobiles; over-powered, torturously uncomfortable and sold without guarantee). But the public always picks itself up. Sooner or later, and usually sooner, it gets its sense of values straightened out.

Just so, if American industry really wants to improve business it will bestir itself in the matter of values. It will not blame organized labor (i.e., uncontrollable labor) for sloppy workmanship in the things it produces, and it will stop cutting costs to increase profits at the expense of quality.

I think a Chevrolet Impala convertible costs about $3,500. Anyway it is advertised, in typical Detroitese, as livable, lovable and luxurious. And last month in California I rented one from Hertz. In Oakland.

Halfway down the block from the garage I realized that it was impossible to use the rear-view mirror because the plastic panel at the back was clouded to the point of opacity. When I took the car back immediately, because I thought it was dangerous to drive, I said to the attendant, "I'm afraid something has happened to this plastic rear window."

"Oh, no," he said, "they all get that way in a month or two."

But, at least, I managed to make a trade for a car where the plastic sheet hadn't gotten so much that way yet; I could make out general shapes bearing down on me.

However, I couldn't use the parking brake. It wouldn't hold.

"Hell, none of them do. Use the gear shift," the Hertz man told me in Monterey.

While I am willing to believe that the brake release handle which came off in my fingers may have been hammered on instead of screwed into place by a disgruntled worker, and so made loose for all time, I am unwilling to believe that Walter Reuther designed the brake that didn't work. Or that a clouded plastic window on a car driven less than 9,000 miles wasn't simply the manufacturer's cheap substitute for the small glass panels that served convertibles admirably for so long.

The Volkswagens and other little foreign cars we see running around must be much less a threat to the American economy than our own failure to offer good values at good prices. When we get back to this fundamental I have no doubt that the success that has always attended it will be with us again.

(Twelve years later the cars that are America's pride and joy still are infected with bugs. On January 22, 1973, General Motors recalled 3.7 million late model Chevrolets, Pontiacs, etc., for a defect that can cause serious accidents, injuries and even

*death, due to malfunctioning of the steering mechanism, which
lacks an 85-cent part.)*

April 11

The other night I read a book about advertising that is likely to be both widely praised and heartily condemned.

It is called *Reality in Advertising* and it was written by
Rosser Reeves, who is chairman of Ted Bates, Inc. David Ogilvy,
Martin Mayer, Ben Sonnenberg and Alfred Politz are loud in
praise of it on the dust jacket, and David Ogilvy says that he is
buying copies for each of his people and each of his clients —
which is surprising because the rules that are set forth are interpreted by the Bates and Ogilvy agencies at opposite ends of
the advertising spectrum.

The book, which is reported to have been written originally
as a Bates presentation, should tell no one in Foote, Cone &
Belding anything new, for at its best it is almost pure Claude
Hopkins and this, as almost everyone knows, is where we
started.

Perhaps it will be most interesting to any of us because,
using the same basic principles, we make advertising that is
usually as different from the Bates product as day is from night.
Bates advertising is built upon what Mr. Reeves calls the Unique
Selling Proposition and he believes in delivering this without
subtlety and without concern for anyone's gentler feelings. He
also proves that such advertising works.

That it may annoy a great many people, he dismisses as
being beside the point.

I don't think this is so.

Dial soap, Clairol, Sunkist, Kleenex, Kotex, Hallmark, Kool-
Aid, Kraft candies, Paper-Mate pens, Klear, Raid, Rheingold
beer, Dole, etc., all are as successful in their highly competitive
fields as any of the Bates-advertised products. All use unique
selling propositions that are as carefully developed and tested
as those that Rosser Reeves points to in the Bates success. But
none uses either jarring or irritating devices, or ugly or ques-
tionable illustrations. We undertake to make advertising that is
a pleasant intruder, if not, indeed, a welcome one.

This, it seems to me, is the only way that advertising can be
done in the public interest. And I don't think anyone else's interest can come first. Whenever it does, advertising is under fire,
and properly so.

Geneva, Switzerland, May 5

It is a warm humid afternoon at the tip end of Lake Geneva . . . and the tip end also of a week that brought us by air from London to Frankfurt and then by car through Weisbaden, Rudesheim, Heidelberg, Basel, Zurich, Lucerne, Bern, Lausanne, and finally, Geneva . . .

Like all of the cities we have seen in Germany and Switzerland, this one has become the site of a curious admixture of old- and new-world architecture: old stone buildings, five or six stories high, with dormer windows jutting out of steep, tile roofs, line block after block; then blocks of severely modern cement buildings, offices and apartments rising somewhat higher, and all sporting balconies, take over until the pattern is reversed. Much as it is in London, Frankfurt, Freiburg, Basel, Zurich and Geneva, all look as if sections of New York or Chicago had been dumped in between the castles and the cathedrals that once were the most distinguishing marks of these cities . . .

The German cities bristle with a kind of grim activity. I was going to say they bustle, but I think this would indicate a lack of order, and this would be wrong. The order is so strict that it seems almost stifling. Germany is not a place for fun. It is all business; and the business is in a hurry.

Our office of 35 people at Rossmarkt 11, in Frankfurt (where I couldn't find a sausage in three good hotels and as many fine restaurants!) is as orderly and as antiseptic-looking as a hospital. Only Don Cunningham and Carl Granath, from Chicago, and Jim Lee, an art director from London, seem truly relaxed in the clean, spacious, tastefully furnished rooms. But then the Frankfurt office got three new accounts within ten days. And taking on Kleenex, Lever's Sunlicht soap, and a new menthol cigarette for the Reynolds affiliate, would probably have made me pretty serious, too.

However, even the people at the Schloss Hotel at Kronberg, which is a one-time castle that belonged to the mother of Kaiser Wilhelm II, where we stayed just outside Frankfurt, were kind of grim.

Someone wrote once that most German people are either at your feet or at your throat. They are either knocking their heels together and saluting, or knocking your head off. I think I felt a kind of inferiority complex that, like most such complexes, manifests itself in a quite opposite approach: shoving you out of the

way at a taxi stand, pushing ahead of you at a dining room en-
trance, even in a first-rate hotel.

One wishes these people could make it, as it were. Then take
life a little bit easier. But this may be impossible. The drive may
be built in and permanent . . .

Over the border at Basel, the grimness disappears. Goodness
knows, the Swiss are not a jolly people, but they are much less
stolid than the Germans, and they are wonderfully polite. They
are surely the most frugal folk I have seen. Two people with
two washbasins and a tub and shower in the very best hotel get
only one tiny cake of soap and nary a match, but this is all
right, for the prices are fair . . .

May 23

The significance in last week's Emmy Awards for the outstanding television programs of 1960 lay not in the considerable
difference between the "ratings" made by the Academy members and those of Nielsen, Trendex and ARB, but rather, I think,
in the impact of these programs on television professionals and
the public alike.

The big winner, of course, was Hallmark's *Macbeth,* which
took the awards for best actor, best actress, best direction, best
drama, and best program of the year.

To these standard awards there was added a new special
one to Mr. J. C. Hall for his staunch backing of programs with
intellectual substance as well as dramatic appeal. It is this
award that was most important of all.

It was ten years ago, half way in our association with Hallmark, that Mr. Hall decided to have no more of traditional programming on regular schedule. While he realized that every
week or every other week television would be important to many
advertisers, it wasn't to Hallmark. Moreover, if he could get out
of this pattern he could afford to do some special programming
that would run to 60 or 90 or even 120 minutes and he could
schedule these programs in connection with Hallmark's peak
selling periods.

With the promise of superior entertainment on his network,
Pat Weaver, who was president of NBC at the time, agreed to
Mr. Hall's proposition, and the Hallmark Hall of Fame has been
scheduled irregularly ever since. This program has won more
awards for artistic endeavor than any other on the air, but the

type of programming has been a means and not an end in itself.

Indeed, it is doubtful if any other series has had the continuous selling force of the Hallmark Hall of Fame.

August 28

Nothing worries some people like advertising. And one of the things they worry about currently is the word *like* in the sentence, *Winston tastes good like a cigarette should.*

"You advertising people," a haughty woman complained to me at dinner one night recently, "stop at nothing. You even corrupt the English language." She was talking about the Winston line. And because I had heard other people objecting to this, too, violently, I decided to look into the matter.

Well, neither the lady at dinner nor any of the other viewers with alarm has much of a leg to stand on.

My Webster devotes thirty-eight lines to examining the word *like* in the precise context of its use by Winston. Examples are given from Shakespeare ("Wishing me like to one more rich in hope"), Keats, Dickens, E. V. Lucas and the King James Bible, before it is stated that this is "common in popular usage but in the works of careful writers (it) is usually replaced by *as*."

This reminds me of Winston Churchill's note to a World War I censor who objected to his ending a sentence with a preposition. Wrote Churchill: "This is the sort of nonsense up with which I will not put."

Mr. Churchill obviously agrees with a famous old English professor of mine that it is only how effectively words work that counts. Popular usage always wins out over old rules in the long run. And so long as advertising people are following Shakespeare I wouldn't think they are trying to shorten the run.

September 5

I am constantly amazed by the gradual discovery, faithfully reported in the advertising trade press, by agency after agency, that this is a creative business.

McCann-Erickson, as you probably know, has gone all out with a special creative group, housed in an ivory tower, separated physically as well as intellectually from the ordinary McCannics, and I read somewhere the other day that this is one of the agency's proudest achievements.

What I couldn't help wondering was whether the pride in

this latest development lies in the experimental decentralization of McCann-Erickson, which has become the most extravagant in the advertising business, or in such fantastic end product as a current Buick headline?

Dynamite from Dreamsville.

This may be creative but it is hardly advertising.

Also I find it hard to fit this abrupt change in Buick's personality with the doctors, lawyers and other conservatives whose preference for Buick has been one of the strongest loyalties in autodom.

Maybe Buick has decided there aren't enough doctors, lawyers and other conservatives any more. Or maybe this is just pretty dopey advertising.

September 19

There is more nonsense talked about creativity in advertising than anything else in the trade since the Townsend brothers' 27 Points in the middle 1930's.

For the most part, creativity in advertising today means anything different from the run of the mill. In print this is generally a matter of graphic presentation. In television it means off-beat.

David Ogilvy started it all with the Hathaway man with the eye patch. Doyle Dane Bernbach carried it along with a campaign in New York newspapers that traded-up Ohrbach's low-priced dress shop with a fine show of sophistication in dramatic photography and shocking headlines. Leo Burnett, at about the same time Hathaway (a very small shirtmaker) emerged from the backwoods of Maine and Ohrbach's began to be fashionable, created the life-size cake and some very convincing "reasons why" Pillsbury's was the best of all mixes.

Following these authentic breakthroughs, almost all of the things that are cited as examples of creativity today turn out to be simply variations on the same themes. The Marlboro man, who has now become also the Alpine man, is actually a tattooed version of the Hathaway man done pretty much in the Ohrbach (or Bernbach) manner.

In the same way, Bernbach's Polaroid camera campaign in print was an adaptation of the technique in Burnett's Pillsbury advertising.

Papert, Koenig, Lois, which *Printers' Ink* classes with

Ogilvy, Bernbach and Burnett for creativity, depends almost solely on variations of the Bernbach layout (four-fifths illustration—even if it's only a single fingernail—and one-fifth text) and way-out contrivances like Wolfschmidt's talking orange.

The misconception of what is truly creative is further illustrated in the current campaign for *The Saturday Evening Post* which fills full newspaper pages with over-size type to present pure rant and fustian.

"Suddenly, The Saturday Evening Post explodes with a blazing new spirit. Color runs riot. Imagination is king. The printed word rises to new glory. A new creative freedom comes to magazines—and the roar of excitement can be heard round the reading and advertising world. Vive la revolution! In the new Saturday Evening Post, suddenly reading becomes a new adventure!"

This puerility is from BBD&O. But it must have been *The Post's* fault. BBD&O does not totally mistake words for ideas.

As for Bernbach, the challenge to be different artistically has brought him to the ultimate: the illustration that is not an illustration. The upper four-fifths of the Volkswagen advertising in this week's *New Yorker* is filled only with a light gray screen. Underneath this nothingness, we read:

"No point showing the '62 Volkswagen. It still looks the same."

Thus does a fine Volkswagen campaign commit absurdity.

The big type for small ideas that characterizes so many current campaigns and the profligate waste of space that uses two pages in a magazine or newspaper to say something that would be of doubtful value in one page had its counterpart in television in the late, loudly lamented Piel's beer commercials in New York. The creative urge was there all right, but the conviction that this must arouse in the advertisee was missing.

Our Clairol and Dial campaigns, our Sunbeam after-shave test, our Kraft barbecue sauce suggestion of outdoor-cooking flavor brought *indoors,* Kool-Aid's smiling pitcher, the new Dole pineapple use recommendations, our Delsey, S.O.S. and Raid television commercials and the basic proposition in our Good Seasons advertising—all these measure up to the true standards of *creative selling,* which is what creative advertising must be if it is to be anything at all.

How do I know this?

For one thing I know the sales figures; I know the standing and the progress of each of these products against the competition.

For another, I know what Leo Burnett is talking about when he speaks of "that wee voice" that guides the creative advertising man.

"In the lonesome caverns of his mind, and in his private viscera, he develops a *thing* of some kind — an idea, a technique, a phrase, a graphic design, whatever. It strikes him as appropriate to the problem he's trying to solve — it seems accurate, and sound, and hopefully *new* and *fresh* and *desirably different*. He may not quite know where it came from, but here he is with a creation."

The key word there, it seems to me, is *appropriate*. And this is what makes good advertising stand out from the foolishness.

September 26

The case against advertising has now been taken up by the British historian, Mr. Arnold Toynbee, and he takes it far beyond the case as presented either by the American historian, Mr. Arthur Schlesinger, Jr., our Ambassador to India, Mr. John Kenneth Galbraith, the pot-boiling Mr. Vance Packard or *Time* magazine.

Indeed, so far does Mr. Toynbee go in condemning "Madison Avenue" for being both un-Christian and un-American that *Time* almost comes to the defense of our business.

In a pamphlet published to reproduce a speech which Mr. Toynbee made at Williamsburg, Virginia, in June, the 72-year-old historian (who recently wrote a whole volume of corrections to an earlier world history) holds that "the tempter's role is being played by everything we sum up under the name of Madison Avenue."

"A considerable part of our ability, energy, time and material resources," he continues, "is being spent today on inducing us to find the money for buying material goods that we should never have dreamed of wanting had we been left to ourselves."

The above, of course, is the Galbraith-Schlesinger line.

Then Toynbee takes off along the Packard path. "The strategy is to try to captivate us without allowing us to become aware of what is being done to us . . . If all else fails (Madison Avenue) will resort to sheer bullying."

Up to this point, I imagine *Time* found the historian on familiar and friendly ground. But then, says *Time*, "Dr. Toynbee reaches a startling conclusion: 'I would suggest that the destiny of our Western Civilization turns on the issue of our struggle with all that Madison Avenue stands for more than it turns on the issue of our struggle with Communism.'"

This even *Time* couldn't take. And while it didn't actually underwrite the answer to the foolish doctor, it does allow the "admen . . . to insist that even the most sophisticated modern advertising cannot artificially create desires, but can only stimulate existing desires by telling people what goods can be had, what they are like, what satisfactions they bring."

What is more important in *Time's* summary of the advertising side is the following:

"Madison Avenue's case for itself closely mirrors the case for free enterprise. It rests on the premise that men have a right to free choice, and given that choice will build themselves a better society than those who have their choices made by others, however high minded."

It is incredible that anyone of Arnold Toynbee's stature could seriously suggest, "Instead of spending our earnings on unwanted consumer goods for ourselves, why not spend them on meeting the basic and pressing needs of the majority of our fellow human beings?"

Where these earnings would come from under some other system of business, and what the majority of our fellow human beings want that is different from what he wants us to give up, Mr. Toynbee fails to point out.

These are the items in our critics' case about which they always are vague. Must it not be that in them lies the collapse of their case?

October 18

There seem to be some misgivings even among our own people about my advocacy of network-programmed television with the rotation of commercials through certain hours of the day and night.

I don't know whether these misgivings arise from a belief

in the networks' avowed inability to work this out on an equitable basis, which seems to me utterly silly (if General Foods or the Johnson Wax people or Procter & Gamble can rotate commercials, I don't know why the networks can't), or whether some of us just love show business so much that we can't let it alone.

In either case, I think there is plenty for us to do in television in making good commercials and in hollering bloody murder about tasteless or shoddy programming. This latter, incidentally, is no more a matter of meddling than when we raise the roof about ugly or sordid or slanted material in magazines or newspapers.

On the other hand, programming should be the network's responsibility just as magazine and newspaper news and features are the editor's responsibility. We should either take it because we like it or leave it because we don't.

It is not only proper that advertisers and their agents should have no part in program planning (except for special programs like Hallmark's or some of Bell & Howell's—lengthy programs of highly intellectual appeal) but it is the only way that the networks can do any serious experimenting. The reason for this should be perfectly clear: you can't ask Johnson's to experiment while competitive Simoniz buys a sure thing.

The risks should be shared. And so should the proved things be open to all advertisers.

On any other basis the advertiser takes all the risk (and gets most of the blame) which alone should be reason enough to want to encourage any system that would change this.

It is reported that 75% of ABC's prime night-time is sold presently in minute spots. NBC is said to be selling 55% this way, and CBS, 25%. The step that I have suggested thus appears to be a very short one to provide more varied entertainment.

It would provide automatic sponsorship for programs of public enlightenment and intellectual stimulation, at the expense only of some tired comedy and worked-over drama.

November 27

A few days ago I had a long letter from Jim Aubrey, president of the CBS Television Network, wherein, amidst a certain amount of head-nodding, he dismissed my proposal that commercials be rotated through most nighttime periods (in programs presented by the networks) as "impractical."

Now I see where another man I regard highly for his knowledge of broadcasting says, even more definitely, "rotation of commercials would be a failure." This is from Edgar Kobak.

On the other hand, magazines as far apart as *Newsweek* and *The New Republic* and *The Saturday Evening Post,* and newspapers as different as *The Christian Science Monitor* and the *New York Herald Tribune,* have found my suggestion more than mildly interesting, for in it they see the only opportunity anyone has conceived of for experimentation in programming, and more intellectual programs, with every advertiser paying his share of the bill.

Incidentally, I contend that an increased number of programs each week devoted to something other than crime and violence and corny comedy might turn on some sets that now are dark, and so increase the advertising value.

However, Messrs. Aubrey and Kobak say no, it can't be done. And NBC and ABC (except for Ollie Treyz) have paid me no attention at all.

It would be easy to decide that they are right and I am wrong, if it weren't for one thing.

The independent British television system operates on almost precisely the basis I have been talking about. Apparently, like the bee who is unaware of the laws of aerodynamics that should keep him from flying, these British broadcasters don't know what they can't do.

1962

March 2

It is one of the favorite fancies of the advertising business to talk about *hot* agencies.

Unfortunately, this often refers to someone who, through exploitation of the Bernbach layout, has done little or nothing more than superimpose headlines on huge illustrations that crowd the type below almost into the margins of magazine or newspaper pages.

In television, the hot designation goes most frequently to agencies whose advertising interpretations are off-beat. (And the more off-beat, the better.)

Mostly, however, the term hot is applied to those agencies that are successful in bagging new accounts in coveys. What isn't so widely publicized is the losses of these so-called hot agencies.

For example, the hottest of them all last year added accounts from five important advertisers. However, this same agency *lost* accounts from five other leading advertisers. Another hot agency added four well-known accounts during the year, but lost eight others whose total dollar value was actually in excess of the additions.

Maybe a cool, steady hand is better to have in the long run than a hot little fist.

March 15

Unfortunately, advertising people, like show people, often become victims of their greatest successes. They get stuck with an image of one kind or another, and instead of wriggling loose they snuggle up to it as if nothing else counted.

Just now, a couple of our better agencies, tagged for originality, suddenly are hell-bent along the comic route. All the evidence that anyone has ever been able to collect indicates that advertising that is made to be clever succeeds only at the expense of the message that it seeks to deliver.

To be clever is bad enough. But to be comic is the worst mistake that anyone can make in advertising. It bears no relationship at all to the gently humorous approach that has marked successful campaigns for such products as Kool-Aid, Jell-O, Sanforizing, etc., in various media.

The difference is that these have made their points by humorous exaggeration, while the comic undertakings usually lampoon the advertising's best prospects or make the product itself a part of the gag rather than an answer for the problem that is presented.

April 11

Media expenditures by Foote, Cone & Belding domestic clients, in 1961, were as follows:

Newspapers	16.0%
Magazines	25.7%
Outdoor	4.2%
Radio	5.6%
Television	48.5%

This week's *Advertising Age* lists the 100 leading magazine advertisers last year, and these include eleven of our clients:

> Armour and Company
> Bristol-Myers Company
> General Foods Corporation
> The Gillette Company
> The B. F. Goodrich Company
> S. C. Johnson & Son, Inc.
> Kimberly-Clark Corporation
> Lever Brothers Company
> National Dairy Products Corporation
> Purex Corporation, Ltd.
> Hiram Walker Incorporated

June 12

I think you will be as surprised as I was by the following book review that Russ Stewart, general manager of the Field newspapers, sent me from *Field and Stream* magazine:

> "Although written many years ago, 'Lady Chatterley's Lover' has just been re-issued by Grove Press, and this fictional account of the day-by-day life of an English gamekeeper is still of considerable interest to outdoorminded readers; as it contains many passages on pheasant raising, the apprehending of poachers, ways to control vermin and other chores and duties of the professional gamekeeper.

> "Unfortunately, one is obliged to wade through many passages of extraneous material in order to discover and savor these highlights on the management of a Midlands shooting estate and, in this reviewer's opinion, this book cannot take the place of J. R. Miller's 'Practical Gamekeeping.' "

So far as book reviews are concerned, I think this will always be my favorite.

June 19

The story in the advertising press that reported our withdrawal from the Tidewater account said something about our "not choosing to be reevaluated." This was not quite right.

Reevaluation in the sense used here (which is one of the new euphemisms of our trade) means that advertisers publicly look over various agencies, even invite solicitations, while keeping the agency of record standing, as it were, with its neck in the noose, waiting for the trap door to drop—or not.

This kind of reevaluation we certainly don't choose to be party to, because it is usually only a prelude to dismissal which we would much prefer to take without the play-acting.

However, there is another kind of continuing reevaluation that we welcome, and we are judged by this by a number of our clients every week.

Armour, for example, retains Young & Rubicam as well as Foote, Cone & Belding, and actually they can compare our operations daily. Clairol has also Doyle Dane Bernbach, and they can do the same thing. General Foods has Benton & Bowles, Ogilvy, Benson & Mather and Young & Rubicam; Johnson has Benton & Bowles and Needham, Louis and Brorby; Kimberly-Clark has William Esty and Doherty, Clifford, Steers & Shenfield; Kraft has Needham, Louis and J. Walter Thompson; Lever has Thompson, BBDO, Sullivan, Stauffer, Colwell & Bayles; Sunkist has Leo Burnett; and so on, to compare with Foote, Cone & Belding.

Since Tidewater had only this agency they couldn't make the same kind of daily or weekly comparison. But they could have talked to these several clients of ours who have an intimate working knowledge of almost all the agencies Tidewater was reported to be talking to in their "reevaluation".

This would have been sensible and understandable, and Tidewater would probably have found out a good deal more about everyone concerned than through presentations—which some of the best agencies make poorly and some pedestrian agencies do very well. The former are usually too busy with their clients to go all out.

June 26

There is a great difference of opinion about the effect of cigaret smoking upon the development of lung cancer. The incidence of heavy smoking has been noted in the history of many stricken people. But the influence of this heavy smoking on the development of the cancer, or whether, in fact, it had any effect at all, has not been established.

If cancer is caused by cigaret smoking, the manufacture and sale of cigarets should be prohibited. Or, if there is a limit within which cigarets are not harmful to most people (as many authorities believe) this should be made known and the manufacturers should be bound to urge that the reasonable limit be observed (as with certain drug products).

It seems to me a suitable undertaking of a government that is as solicitous as ours of the welfare of people all over the globe to put whatever effort is necessary into a search for the truth in this matter, then act accordingly.

Meanwhile I am entirely out of sympathy with an action by the American Cancer Society to prevent the advertising of cigarets on television broadcasts of college football games. According to the *Chicago Daily News* (Saturday, June 23) the A.C.S. is urging that letters be sent to the heads of 100 colleges and universities asking them to "conscientiously" consider the effects of such sponsorship.

Whatever the effects of the sponsorship might be, this action of the Society is unwarranted and audacious. So long as it is legal to make and sell cigarets it should be proper to advertise them. To strike at a business by attempting to curtail its promotion by petition and by pressure is undeniable coercion.

Incidentally, if the Society seriously wants to discourage the sale of cigarets to young people, which I believe is illegal in most states, it would do well to look into the distribution of cigarets through vending machines which make them available to anyone.

(Little did I dream that cigaret advertising would be removed from the airwaves but allowed to appear without restraint in magazines and newspapers.

(It is either harmful to smoke cigarets or it is harmless, at least to smoke in moderation, and advertising should be regulated accordingly and for all media alike.)

July 3

It is one of the strongest beliefs of some advertising critics that non-advertising, which may be either a parody of real advertising or an off-beat comic substitute, is much to be preferred over the real thing.

One of the leading exponents of non-advertising is an amusing fellow named Stan Freberg whose Chun King television commercials, bought through Batten, Barton, Durstine & Osborn, have been a sensation with the cult.

BBDO, which should have known better than to monkey with non-advertising in the first place, recently was fired by Chun King which, nevertheless, retained Freberg.

Anyway, this is to report a victory for one of our clients over the comic. Stan Freberg's *"Does she or doesn't she use Chun King Chow Mein? Only her grocer knows for sure"* was quite understandably objected to by Clairol. Now Clairol has been upheld by ABC where the commercial was scheduled.

I have no doubt this will be cited in the annals of advertising as gross and exaggerated lack of sympathy with a creative artist. (Indeed, *Newsweek* is already hooting.) But it is my own conviction that Freberg is not only a non-advertising man but also a non-artist. The thing is, his lines would have been meaningless if Clairol hadn't spent millions of dollars establishing *"Does she . . . or doesn't she? Only her hairdresser knows for sure,"* for hair color rinse.

September 7

For a long time *Grey Matter,* the monthly letter of Grey Advertising, Inc., has offered stimulating thoughts and ideas on advertising and marketing.

The most recent issue encloses a reproduction from the advertising column in *The New York Times* that calls proud attention to the shift of a fairly important account from another agency to Grey.

What the story fails to relate is that Grey hired the long-time account supervisor from the other agency, and that he began what proved to be a successful campaign to switch the business, claiming that he had been responsible for the old agency's good work.

This is the kind of thing that discredits the entire advertising business.

I hope we will continue to hire people because we want *them* and not for any business on which they may be thought to have an inside track. In the course of the last twenty years I believe I have turned down two dozen men "with an account" and I trust we will never change this rule.

October 12

I pass along to you the following from Ernie Eversz:

"Timothy Howley, a new young writer with us, just showed me an obscure, but very charming book, 'The Inside Story of Adam and Eve' by Edward S. Jordan. He ran across it because of his interest in early automobiles and the author happens to be the Jordan of the Jordan car.

"Some of the things Mr. Jordan had to say in 1945 about advertising are, of course, still true today, but it is the saltiness of his expressions that is so interesting.

"For instance, in the foreword he explains how he learned about advertising and attributes his knowledge to his mother in this way: 'I learned about *people* from her,' said Jordan, 'and that knowledge is vital to good advertising. She never used the word Psychology, but she did say that "Tillie Hart wound up at that Devil Creek place because she valued silk stockings above her immortal soul" . . . while . . . "Mrs. Webster's Fred has been raised to five dollars a day, so she is trying to learn to like olives and read a book." '

"Later he speaks about advertising, which I think is pretty interesting: God has endowed a few men and women with a spirit that rings in their written words, but they must know and *believe* that the words they are writing are *so*. You can 'make' a few pretty good advertising 'experts' but the results will be synthetic. You couldn't *hire* a Moses to inscribe the best piece of copy ever produced—the Ten Commandments; train a Lincoln by mail to write the next best, the Gettysburg Address; ghost-write Ike Eisenhower into the 'Abilene Paragraph' which flashed from London into the hearts of all true Americans.

" 'That Priceless Ingredient: Integrity' that Raymond Rubicam found in Squibbs has always been dominant in Rubicam himself. Ted MacManus, who wrote *The Penalty of Leadership* for Cadillac, believed with all his Celtic soul that it was *so*.

"Another observation of Jordan's which I think is of particular significance in this day of shoddy merchandise is: 'Once a man assumes the obligation of living up to his advertising, his product must constantly be made better than he says it is, or he will eventually fail, while his success inspires others to efforts to improve upon what he has done.' "

November 6

It is the bitter complaint of most critics of our American economic system that our production and consumption of a vast total of unnecessary, or luxury, goods is immoral and debilitating.

Before this new anguish became fashionable in certain academic circles, and particularly at Harvard University, critics of the same baleful fraternity worried mostly because the fruits of our enterprise were not equally distributed among all people; and they went all out for almost any socialistic suggestion that would change this.

Now that the socialist societies have failed monumentally to achieve Utopia and, in fact, lag far behind ours in producing even the necessities of life for their masses, the apostles of apprehension have decided that the wealth our people share, in terms of unnecessities, is something to be forever shunned.

How wrong these people are can easily be demonstrated by asking this question: where would the money come from to finance our national defense without the taxes on payrolls and profits that our production of non-necessities supports? Also, one might ask: how is our population to be engaged, if it is not to produce new automobiles, television receivers, power lawn mowers, cake mixes, cosmetics and all the host of other things that Americans are said to be improperly induced to want and to buy?

The answer to both these questions, of course, is that the widespread purchase and pleasurable use of such clearly non-necessities as musical instruments, record players, cleansing tissues, greeting cards, nylon stockings, electric blankets, pretty china and glass ware, and so on and on, are measurements not only of affluence but also of a civilization that refuses to return to the level of the ox-powered farm.

I know this because I have just been out looking at it. I have been exploring a group of new, large Montgomery Ward retail stores in Fort Worth and Dallas, Texas, in connection with a directors meeting that was held at the Fort Worth mail order and catalog house. The latter is a building containing 1.5 million feet and it is filled with goods that make no other contribution to living than to help make it easier, more comfortable and more exciting.

Despite the men of Harvard (and Oxford, I am afraid) I couldn't possibly have felt less guilty, either as a director of Ward's or as a participant in our economy, than in that huge storehouse of luxuries, which is one of nine around the U. S.

within which Ward's $1.3 billion of 1962 sales will be expedited. Three hundred patterns in carpet is an example of the choice Ward's makes available by mail order and through its 525 retail stores and its 640 catalog stores. The number of items in stock is in excess of one hundred thousand!

Perhaps the most astonishing (non-philosophical) thing about the mail order house is the fact that simply by weighing the mail as it comes in at four, six and seven o'clock each weekday morning it is possible to know almost exactly what the volume will be in each of the eighty-odd departments that day; order clerks are deployed like troops as a result. Many of these wear skates; supervisors ride bicycles. And I hope Vance Packard never sees them, for this is a business of fantastic proportions.

John Kenneth Galbraith and Dr. Arnold Toynbee would find it equally depressing.

A single popcorn machine in the candy department in the retail store attached to the Fort Worth mail order house sells $35,000 worth of freshly popped and buttered popcorn every year! Each of the Fort Worth and Dallas retail stores bores finger grips in bowling balls to measure, and sells dozens every week. One of the largest departments in each of the five stores I visited is the toy department. Excellent reproductions of fine paintings are another luxury by any count. Wigs are a current rage, selling at $3.98 to $155, and selling in the thousands.

Montgomery Ward's new stores (like Sears') are large, light, airy, neat and clean, and filled with shoppers — mostly, during the daytime store hours, women with children, having a ball; looking at things, asking questions, learning the difference between good, better and best wherever there are grades; happily, and with no trepidation, buying obvious non-necessities.

The notion that these people are constantly flim-flammed and sold shoddy goods to exploit their shamefully synthesized wants is the purest humbug. Messrs. Galbraith, Toynbee, Packard, et al., are only high-domed misanthropes. They don't want popcorn, candy, lipstick, sports coats, power tools, rubber plants, parakeets, dolls, wigs, fur-trimmed coats, boats, or such, for themselves, so they decry these things for everybody else.

Their compassion for the people they cry over is only a mask for the contempt they feel for fun.

December 7

It will be known by everyone who receives this memo that I have no axe to grind for the cigaret industry; it is now more than ten years since our parting with The American Tobacco Company and our only connection with cigaret makers today is with Reynolds, in Germany.

Nevertheless, I deplore the proposal by LeRoy Collins, president of the National Association of Broadcasters, that they include special tobacco industry advertising standards in their radio and television codes. Gov. Collins is a friend of mine, and I generally agree with his views of business conduct. But this time I feel that he is looking from a sentimental point of view, and not seeing what he suggests in the light of good judgment.

I have mentioned before that various propositions that would constrict cigaret advertising are contrary to the basic concept of our free choice society. This is not to argue for a minute that cigarets may not be harmful when smoked in some as yet undetermined numbers over an equally undetermined period of time.

What it is to say, as I have said before, is that so long as the government cannot make up its mind about the dangers in cigaret smoking, and so long as there is no prohibition and no limitation of cigaret manufacture and sale there should be no prohibition and no limitation of cigaret advertising by any other means than industry agreement to exercise reasonable restraint.

Such reasonable restraint would apply to advertising illustrations (in print or in television) that might glorify very young smokers or urge their emulation of popular and presumably infallible public figures; i.e., the Green Bay half-back, Mr. Paul Hornung, who lights up a Marlboro on television almost every hour on the hour, all through the long Fall weekends.

The glorification of youthful smokers depends upon one's idea of age, I suppose, and while the dreamy dolls who blow Pall Mall smoke skyward from green grassy dells seem terribly young to me, they may appear almost ancient to teen-agers. So, just here, we have one of the problems with advertising codes: how would Gov. Collins write this one, who would be the arbiters of age, and would this be based on the calendar or the camera?

Martin Mayer, who wrote *Madison Avenue, U.S.A.*, also has entered the argument, with the opinion that "Mr. Collins is dead right" in taking "the initiative" in the tobacco-cancer dispute. Mr. Mayer, like Gov. Collins, is confusing the responsibilities of advertising and manufacturing, and in trying to get at the latter through the former he is side-stepping the real issue, which should be to determine what the limits are at which cigaret smoking becomes harmful and see to it that these are made known.

That some people who have smoked heavily have become victims of lung cancer is a fact. But it is also a fact that millions of people who smoke moderately have not developed cancer. What we need is more information on the subject of cigarets and not legislation (industry-wise or otherwise) to cut down smoking by arbitrarily restricting advertising. If Gov. Collins is successful in this endeavor there is no reason why someone else should not undertake to restrict some other advertising for almost any quixotic reason.

Dr. Persia Campbell, as a case in point, points sadly to the expenditure of $300 million annually by eighteen million teenagers for cosmetics. Dr. Campbell is an economist at Queens College, in New York, and a lecturer on New York City's new educational television station. She is charming and effective; and, in my opinion, very wrong in at least part of her concern for these young people.

By doing a little simple arithmetic, I have discovered that Dr. Campbell's distress with these millions of boys and girls and the millions they spend upon such unnecessities, is concerned with an expenditure of less than five cents per day, for lipstick, nail polish, hair rinse, hair tonic, after-shave lotion, deodorants, etc., that make them neater, cleaner, and more attractive than any other teen-agers ever were before.

Besides, whatever else could anyone do with 4.5 cents per day?

They couldn't buy many cigarets.

1963

Carmel, Calif., March 5

The other day I was invited to participate in a nation-wide television program as a panelist who would speak for advertising.

Through the years I have put up my share for the defense

of advertising. I have done this in speeches in more than thirty cities, and by a number of magazine and newspaper articles and radio and television appearances.

Now I have decided to say no more.

The number of pure fakers in the business probably isn't very great, and advertising is a means they use because it is the cheapest way of establishing their contacts with their prey; it is not the nature of advertising to live in dark alleys.

Of course, any sensible person knows this. Most of the arguments against advertising are silly on any other basis than that these are really arguments against the kind of society that must rely on continuous selling pressure to keep its economy in high. Perhaps our economy is wrong. But advertising derives from it, not the other way around.

So much for the philosophy.

The worst thing about advertising is some of the things that are said in its behalf. And the worst of these are about the great discoveries that are made from time to time of new means for making it fool-proof.

I came into the business at about the time two nondescript brothers named Townsend were peddling 27 secret check points with which they promised to evaluate copy and separate the chaff from the wheat. (Appropriately enough, one of their first sales was made to the Quaker Oats Company.) Anyway, the Townsends raised a lot of hell; like most of the advertising witch doctors they insisted upon excluding the agencies from their seances, and under these circumstances there is always a period of name calling and other minor bubblings of bad feeling before the gurus are sent back to the hills.

I have assisted in this, too.

After the Townsends there was the army of European and other mercenaries made up like sociologists, psychologists, psychiatrists and even hypnotists that tried to make a killing out of why people did things everyone knew they did and had no reason to care why. The "why" led to the real swindle the professors perpetrated, which was their guarantee to manufacture motives. This went along for several years and took in some pretty bright advertisers and agents who wanted to be in the swing, and spawned the fictions of Vance Packard and John Kenneth Galbraith to plague them ever since.

Recently these arch foes of advertising (and the system of

which it is a part) have been given very little new to feed on.

Up to last week, that is.

Now one of the agencies has announced the perfection of a device which measures the relative flick of the eyes that is caused by different degrees of interest in different pictures. One discovery that was hailed in the account I saw was that photographs cause more flicker than drawings where the subject is the same.

I pass this on to you because I think you should know that an agency invention has now proved something that everyone I have known in advertising during the last thirty years has been aware of.

As long as advertising people fool around with such monkey business, they will need all the apologists they can find.

But they can't have me any more.

I am going to be too busy nursing my intuition.

May 15

Peter Bart, in yesterday's *New York Times,* quoted the president of a "vast advertising agency" as insisting that "an ad agency is simply a 'super-market' in which a client can purchase whatever advertising he wishes for whatever product. 'We can't sit in judgment on our clients,' he declares."

Well, I have no idea who it is that Peter Bart quotes, and I shall withhold any comment that might be considered a moral criticism.

On the other hand, I believe that an advertising agency that refuses to sit in everlasting judgment on its clients is headed inevitably toward failure. Wrong-minded advertisers ruin good advertising people; they make them cynical, and in the long run, worthless to good business. Moreover, good advertisers are learning to keep strictly away from advertising agencies that serve doubtful clients; the service to the former may depend entirely upon the mood of the latter, as all of us have seen. When the bad client kicks up, the result is like a toothache: only one tooth may have anything wrong with it, but the pain rages all through the mouth.

I do not contend that agencies should exercise any more judgment on their clients than the clients do upon the agencies. But I think the exercise should be equal and continuous.

Only thoughtful advertisers and conscientious advertising

people working together have any chance of lasting accomplishment. For either partner in such an association to leave all judgment to the other is both foolish and dangerous.

It is one of the most important of the agency's functions to contribute experience with many clients to the problems of each one. Thus, for an advertiser to ignore such experience, or for an agency to withhold it, out of deference or out of fear, would seem to suggest a badly mistaken arrangement.

June 3

There are a good many things people (even business people) don't know either about advertising or about advertising agencies.

Their lack of understanding of advertising itself may be seen at any hour of the day or night on television, or in any magazine or newspaper, where the very first rules of advertising are flouted and the only value that is present is whatever return may be had from name repetition. A great deal of this advertising implies a belief on the part of the advertiser that all America is waiting to see and hear what he has to say. For the most part, most of America couldn't care less (except about food products) at any given time.

Good advertising seeks out its interested prospects and talks to them reasonably and persuasively in their own selfish interest. It doesn't scream, it isn't off-beat, and it doesn't use a picture of a dog or a baby to lead into a story about non-skid tires (that will keep you from running over a dog in the rain); or an electric shaver (that will make your face as smooth as a baby's).

Good advertising means telling someone who has a reason to be interested, something he or she ought to know. And if it is "she" it had better be businesslike, even if the business is beauty. No one has yet developed better judgment than the average woman standing in the middle of a supermarket thinking about spending her money. Compositely, she is the world's leading economist, and she is not going to be led into foolishness by any (repeat any) advertising. She may be cheated once in a while, but she always gets even. She not only refuses to buy the fooler-product a second time, but she tells everyone within earshot what is the matter with it.

(There is one exception. Although 60 per cent of women say

they think cosmetics advertising is a cross between wild exag-
geration and pure fiction, they support it as one of their greatest
indulgences, and with their eyes wide open. It is almost as if
there were a happy conspiracy to create a second life and char-
acter for the hard-boiled shopper in the supermarket.)

October 21

This is a repetition of something that has been said many
times before in our business, but evidence is all around us that
failure to follow any one of the basic principles of advertising
inevitably results in something ranging downward from near
miss to sheer disaster.

Most misadventures in advertising by good people probably
are attributable to the mistake that is easiest of all to make,
which is designing an advertisement instead of planning a
proposition; and not even the best advertising people, in the best
agencies, working for the best advertisers, are able always to
resist this impulse.

There are no better advertising people around than those
who work for Mr. Bernbach, Mr. Burnett and Mr. Ogilvy.

Nevertheless, Mr. Bernbach's people lately have been guilty
of such advertisingese as an advertisement for Rival dog food,
entitled "Funny that fat people have fat dogs." Mr. Burnett's
people are responsible for a magazine campaign for Motorola
television that features a series of highly improbable designs
for houses. And Mr. Ogilvy's people have managed an advertisement for Sears color TV that is illustrated with a striking color
photograph of three children, in rapt attention — to something
entirely offstage.

All of these are unique advertisements, I suppose, and if
one is a connoisseur of advertising, noteworthy for their techni-
cal excellence. On the other hand, if one is only mildly interested
in advertising, as ninety out of a hundred people are, but reasonably alert to important product practices, as almost all people are, then I submit that Rival advertising might better talk
entirely about fat dogs, Motorola about television performance
and cabinetry, and Sears about the reliability that is built into
its Silvertone sets.

Obviously, I am much more interested in Zenith television
than in Motorola or Sears television, and I am pleased to believe
that most advertisements for Zenith TV, like the Zenith sets

themselves, are superior. Also, I am not just about to brazen out advice to our confreres. My only suggestion is to ourselves to make no similar mistakes. Actually, Rival does talk about fat dogs (and what overweight means in canine terms), Motorola does talk about beautiful pictures and beautiful cabinets — and even adds a full year's warranty, and Sears does talk reliability. But neither headline nor illustration, in any of these advertisements, helps in any way to make its basic promise clear.

And to be clear, let us remind ourselves, is the very first rule of good advertising: *to be clear what the product promise is, to be clear what the advertiser is really talking about, to be clear why it is in the reader's own best selfish interest to pay attention.*

Let us remember that picturing fat owners of fat dogs may be fun, but advertising isn't. Let us bear in mind that illustrations in print, like pictures in television, are only as good as what they say clearly. And let us keep it also in mind that headlines should support illustrations and vice versa, just as the words in television should always apply to the picture on the screen . . .

1964

January 27

There is no announcement we ever make that is made with greater reluctance or more unhappily than when we must announce the ending of a client relationship.

Usually such announcements are made without comment, except to express our regret.

The notice of our termination by Lever Brothers Company in the United States does, however, call for some explanation. For the end that is coming May 1 to this long-time association was not desired by either of us. It is entirely a matter of circumstances that results from the complexities in a number of our other client assignments.

Current commitments make it impossible for us to serve Lever Brothers in any of several areas they are presently exploring. Such exploration can only be carried out under present circumstances by other Lever agencies; and without the income from Pepsodent and Imperial Margarine advertising to help offset their costs, this is very expensive.

Hence the appointment of Sullivan, Stauffer, Colwell & Bayles for Pepsodent, and Ogilvy, Benson & Mather for Imperial. Both of these are long-time Lever agencies, and we can only wish that both these new assignments result in great success for everyone concerned.

There hasn't been any other dentifrice than Pepsodent in my house for thirty years, and I expect to keep it there. Imperial Margarine, too.

April 27

Books about advertising are nothing new. But the ones that are worth anything are very few.

Rosser Reeves' *Reality in Advertising,* published in 1961, caused a minor sensation when the marketing director of the Mobiloil company read it and immediately switched that company's advertising to the Ted Bates agency of which Reeves was chairman.

Actually, the Reeves book was simply a reproduction in hard covers of the standard Bates solicitation, and the philosophy of advertising which it espoused under the banner of realism seemed to a good many people to be inexcusably ugly. Reeves cynically called advertising "the art of getting a unique selling proposition into the heads of the most people at the lowest possible cost," and I suppose his Anacin television commercials with bells ringing and hammers pounding in the boxes of a man's brain are a fair example.

Mobiloil, incidentally, is advertised primarily in terms of "megatane ratings" which were invented in the Bates copy department.

Following Rosser Reeves' revelations, I suppose it was inevitable that David Ogilvy, who disagrees with Reeves on almost every point, should render his standard solicitation into book form. And he did this with style and some fine anecdotes in his *Confessions of an Advertising Man* last Fall. Ogilvy's book became a best seller because the book is about Ogilvy the advertising man, done with humor and enormous enthusiasm for the subject, and not really about advertising at all.

To be sure, there is a good deal of talk in the *Confessions* about the advertising agency business, but this is something else.

Advertising is usually interesting to read about only when its villainous uses are described, as in *The Hucksters* or *The*

Hidden Persuaders, which are almost equally works of fiction, or
E. S. Turner's *Shocking History of Advertising* (1952) in which
some hundreds of years of advertiser misdeeds were exhumed
and bitterly attacked. For this reason I have declined invitations
from several large publishers to reply (a) to Rosser Reeves and
(b) to David Ogilvy. I have written a good many words about
advertising and I may still undertake a book some day.

Meanwhile, I find the villainies in this business not only unpleasant but also dreadfully repetitious. They are fixed in human
nature, and advertising is only one of many endeavors in which
bad manners and bad morals are in competition with decency.
But I don't want to argue this; it should have become clear
long ago.

On the other side, on the good side of advertising, I am in
sharp disagreement with Rosser Reeves' hard-boiled approach
which sounds for all the world like Joseph Goebbels: "In the
long run only he will achieve basic results in influencing public
opinion who is able to reduce problems to the simplest terms
and who has the courage to keep forever repeating them in this
simplified form despite the objections of the intellectuals."

The quotation is from Goebbels' diary.

Reeves sees himself as something of a latter day Claude
Hopkins, and perhaps he is. David Ogilvy, rather more pleas-
antly, views himself as the incomparable Ogilvy, and this can
get a little bit sticky. Ogilvy, in his *Confessions,* lists seven separate sets of rules for guaranteeing excellence in advertising.
These cover campaign planning, writing headlines, writing copy,
layout and illustration, and specifically, the creation of food,
travel and proprietary medicine advertising.

Ogilvy is a compulsive compiler. Altogether, he sets down
eighty rules in the categories listed here, and while I can (and
do) accept much of his philosophy (since it is largely mine,
too), I think David Ogilvy's finest advertisements could have
been made with no more than five basic rules:

1) Advertising should be entirely clear (as to what
   the proposition is).
2) The proposition should be complete (there should
   be no serious question left unanswered).
3) Advertising should seek its logical prospects (it
   should never try to talk to everyone).
4) Advertising should make a contribution all by it-

self (its prospects should learn something from it, or be usefully reminded of something by it).

5) The aim of advertising is an immediate favorable decision (to do something reasonable that the advertising calls for).

There are obviously certain circumstances or environments in which these rules work best. Advertising is something you do when you can't make an offer face to face. It is a substitute for personal salesmanship. Thus you try to give it a good salesman's attractive appearance, good manners, and flair. The story you have to tell may or may not be demonstrable. When it is, advertising comes easily; when it isn't, good advertising is harder to come by.

Nevertheless, the above are the vital rules, and they apply equally to all product or service advertising in all media at all times.

Anyone could pick out of television or print examples of success and failure every day that are plainly the result of the attention that is paid (or not paid) to these simple admonitions. All are accounted for in every successful advertisement; at least one is ignored in every failure.

The following from recent issues of *The New Yorker* are typical of the befuddlement in which some advertising people live. I defy anyone to tell me what these headlines mean:

The trouble with drinking
champagne ordinarily is,
you have to organize it
like bridge or touch
(Paul Masson)

Not every man who wears GGG clothes
is the captain's captain
(GGG)

He hates caviar, too!
(Guinness)

At 8:15 A.M. Walter Goodman's wife served him his
first pure cup of Brazilian coffee. After one taste, he
leaned over and kissed her. By the time he left for
work, Walter Goodman had agreed to new living room
drapes, 5 Basa Nova lessons, and another small loan
till his brother-in-law, Sheldon, finds himself. Man . . .
that's coffee.   (Coffee of Brazil)

Show me a woman who won't flirt ...
and I'll show you a woman
who probably won't enjoy Italy!

(Alitalia)

Don't bother going to Buenos Aires
to keep up with the Joneses
(They haven't been there yet)

(Panagra)

What I may decide to do one of these days is analyze a hundred or so successful campaigns according to the rules outlined here and show how really good advertising people are undeviating in their adherence to them. Actually, these rules are all I know about making advertisements, and even with examples they would make a thin book.

Also, I am afraid that it would serve no good purpose. The temptation to experiment will always lead the majority of advertising people astray.

They are essentially fun-loving and, unhappily, they mostly want to play.

The foregoing was prompted by reading an excellent new book on the morality of advertising called *Advertising. A New Approach,* by Walter Taplin, whose new approach is to brush aside all the standard arguments about advertising, both pro and con, and look at it for what it is.

Taplin is a British editor and teacher (London School of Economics) whose understanding of the principle of human wants he attributes to the writings of Frank H. Knight, professor emeritus in the Division of Social Sciences at the University of Chicago.

"Most conscious desire," said Knight, "is ultimately a wish to play a role, to be some kind of person in some kind of human world." Then he added that wants themselves are affected by the economic arrangements that are made to meet them. Taplin's conclusion is that advertising is simply the means by which some of these arrangements are made known.

I guess I wish that someone would be as convincing about method in advertising as Taplin is in justifying it in the scheme of things.

Reeves and Ogilvy have given virtuoso performances. But this is not enough.

May 12

I believe I was one of the first people in advertising to applaud the bright, understated copy and the striking layouts that came out of Doyle Dane Bernbach.

The Ohrbach department store advertisements set the pace, in New York City newspapers. Then came the Volkswagen series in magazines; and these and the demonstrations in print for Polaroid are in my list of great campaigns.

But something has happened to the people who made that advertising.

It began with the Avis series which constituted a direct attack on Hertz rent-a-car service. This implied that Hertz cars were less clean than Avis cars and Hertz people less courteous and less concerned for their customers than Avis people; for while Hertz wasn't named, there was clearly no one else for No. 2 Avis to be challenging for first place.

Aggressive solicitation is understandable. This is what advertising is for. But when it takes the form of denigration I think it is badly conceived and deplorable — however cleverly it may be done.

Another unpleasant example of this concept is the current campaign for American Airlines which has suggested subtly, but unmistakably, that only American's fan-jets are really safe to fly in.

"They get you off the ground a full third of a mile sooner than ordinary jets.

"And they get you up in the clear a good 30% faster.

"American Airlines has the largest fan-jet fleet in the world. *In fact, fan-jets are the only jets we'd take you up in.*"

(Italics are mine)

For Olin, which owns Squibb, we are treated to the complaint that "everybody and his brother is trying to make an electric tooth brush" including "shaver manufacturers. And mixer manufacturers."

Thus, what seems to Avis most admirable, seems to Olin very wrong, for Squibb introduced the automatic tooth brush in 1960, and Sunbeam (shaver manufacturer) and General Electric (mixer manufacturer) are tagged as johnny-come-latelies. The fact of the matter, of course, is that G.E. and Sunbeam were making electric appliances back when Squibb was failing in the tooth paste business.

Consistency has no place in this new pattern.

Nor, it appears, has old-fashioned honesty.

The following is from Rival for its new Medium Rare Dog Food.

"There is nothing like Medium Rare on the market. It actually looks as good, smells as good and tastes as good as people-food. As it should. Medium Rare is *nothing but beef chunks, fifteen juicy ounces of beautiful, well-marbled chunks of radiant-broiled beef.*"

Actually, the chunks are manufactured from ground beef and beef by-products, which are the organs that can be lifted out of an animal and are not connected to bone; they are non-muscle meat and consist of lungs, liver, heart, stomach, etc. Other ingredients in Medium Rare include ground beef bone, corn meal, wheat flour, soy bean meal, salt, sodium nitrate and water sufficient for processing.

Beautiful, well marbled, radiant-broiled beef, indeed.

What a promise to make to the President's new Consumer Committee!

Carmel, Calif., July 10

When Foote, Cone & Belding was founded, on January 2, 1943, the United States was engaged in war in many places, and business and advertising were two of its minor concerns.

Other than two or three long stories in *Advertising Age,* which covered the liquidation of the venerable Lord & Thomas and the emergence of the tyro Foote, Cone & Belding in its place in considerable detail (and with rather remarkable accuracy judged by today's penchant for speculation) there was little in the press to suggest that the new agency had any likelihood of succeeding to the position of the old one.

As a matter of fact, *Time* magazine dismissed the whole thing by remarking archly that "changing the name of Lord & Thomas to Foote, Cone & Belding was like changing the name of Tiffany to Smith, Jones & Brown," and that seemed to settle the matter. Nor am I about to reopen it. My purpose here is something different.

Despite the general disinterest in agency matters in 1943 (there were no newspaper advertising columns then) the unusual circumstances of the founding of the company seemed to offer an opportunity to Paul West, president of the Association of National Advertisers, to come up with a new speaker at the annual meeting of the A.N.A. He reasoned that the advertising managers would want to see what kind of men had thrown away the great name of Lord & Thomas and substituted their own. This, of course, was not really an issue; we had wished for the old name above everything else, but Albert Lasker, who owned it, decided otherwise. He felt that the name was synonymous with his own and that the two should go into retirement together.

Anyway, Paul West invited me to address the A.N.A. convention (on the subject of advertising responsibility), which I did in April, 1943, at the Pennsylvania Hotel in New York. And I have been talking about advertising responsibility ever since. The talks have had various titles, but they have really had only one theme: what advertising is and how it should be made in the twin interests of the decent advertiser and his public, which I hold to be identical . . .

The discussion of creativity in advertising has got down to a wrangle between certain of the followers of Mr. Bernbach, who feel that arriving at a reasonable selling proposition for a product only begins the advertising job, and who are more or less willing to scrap the selling proposition if there is any way to get more attention, and the supporters of Mr. Burnett and Mr. Ogilvy (of whom I am one) who believe that if the product is made interesting, the advertising will be interesting in the only way that makes the slightest bit of difference.

This latter group believes there is drama in every product, and that the advertising man's problem is to find it; the former thinks the drama is *added* by advertising. Just so, you have advertisements from the Burnett, Ogilvy, Foote, Cone & Belding side that have headlines like the following:

Quick-cooked Niblets Corn has
everything a fresh young roasting ear has
except the cob

At 60 miles an hour the loudest noise in this
new Rolls Royce comes from the electric clock

Aren't you glad you use Dial Soap?
Don't you wish everybody did?

And from the "new school":

Lemon

He hates caviar, too!

It makes the commercials smaller

The "lemon" is a Volkswagen that failed to pass inspection. The man who "hates caviar, too!" probably won't like Guinness Stout, either. What "makes the commercials smaller" is a Sony miniature television set that makes the programs much smaller by the same token.

There can't be any doubt that each of these is an arresting headline. But the first three pick out logical prospects with crystal-clear propositions in which a promise is inherent, while the second group undertakes to attract attention simply by being off-beat. As a result, each of the first three is successful. Two of the second three fail to pick out anyone and thus must be considered failures (except, perhaps, as entertainment — which should not be advertising's role); and "Lemon" only makes sense in the context of some scores of Volkswagen advertisements done with a similar reverse twist.

I suppose what I want to say is that I believe most people in advertising will do better to follow the Burnett-Ogilvy-FC&B line than the Bernbach one. The latter requires a Bernbach at the wheel; just now there is only one and he is pretty busy; moreover, the Bernbach ploy doesn't always work. (I hate to mention the Rival dog food campaign again, but you just can gussy-up advertising too much.)

There is nothing in the current discussion, which was featured last week in the serious pages of *Dun's Review,* that suggests the slightest change in the five basic rules for making advertising:

1. Make it clear (what the proposition is).
2. Make it complete (what the promise is).
3. Make it important.
4. Make it personal (who is the promise important to?).
5. Make it demanding (that some action be taken) . . .

(I see that this is the third time these rules have been repeated in these pages. But I make no apology. They can't be repeated too often, for they are the sinews of advertising.)

Carmel, Calif., July 21

The greatest problem in advertising today, and it is growing, is the tendency of corporations large and small to do away with skilled advertising people in favor of marketing men who, while intelligent and hard-working, are often so involved with product development, packaging, pricing, broker-relations, sales coverage, etc., that they have little or no time left for the exercise of considered advertising judgment. This is left to the agencies, except that the agencies in their time are accountable in increasing degree to the witch doctors. Nor do all agencies resent this; escape from responsibility is almost irresistible in a business where no one knows anything for sure.

Or don't they? . . .

This brings us back to the simplest and most effective of all headline tests, or tests of opening remarks in television commercials: *Could you say it to a friend without feeling like an idiot?*

If you could, it will probably be effective, and needs no testing, unless it contains only one of several reasonable approaches. If the latter is the case, one should always test for the best . . .

*

Just here it might be well to remind ourselves also that how a promise is made is almost as important in advertising as what the promise is. In conversation this isn't terribly important. In advertising it may be vital. In conversation you may change your stance and start over again. In advertising you get only a fleeting opportunity.

This is another place where advertising sense and sensibility pay big dividends, and they should never be subjected to the ritual of the seance.

The right order of words comes from people who have lived with words for a long time, happily and successfully, just as the right kind of advertising promises come from people who have built these into winning products. Neither are either manufactured according to formula nor wrung out of reluctant respondents in unnatural settings.

I have quoted the famous lines:

"With men who know tobacco best —
with independent auctioneers, buyers and warehousemen,
It's Luckies 2 to 1!"

Try it this way:

"Independent tobacco experts —
auctioneers, buyers and warehousemen —
choose Luckies 2 to 1."

Or this way:

"We choose Luckies 2 to 1 —
say independent auctioneers, buyers and warehousemen,
the world's greatest tobacco experts."

Mr. Hill never bought a headline (or a tagline) that didn't
have a ringing rhythm, that didn't scan. "Nature in the raw is
seldom mild — Smoke Lucky Strike, it's toasted." "Reach for a
Lucky instead of a sweet." "L/S/M/F/T. Lucky Strike means
fine tobacco." "With men who know tobacco best, etc."

Not all the searching of all the serious advertising search-
ers, from my old friend Ernest Dichter to my somewhat newer
friend Leo Shapiro, has turned up anything so important as the
things that competent advertising people know instinctively.

Unfortunately, there aren't nearly enough of these to go
around, and so we have headlines like the following:

As little as $50*
takes you to Europe first class
on the fabulous
S.S. FRANCE
*If you are a dog accompanied by a human.
Humans pay slightly more.

On television we have the dames who would rather fight
than switch from Tarryton and inevitably get a shiner for
their pains.

And this is advertising?

August 12

We live in a time and place where warnings of all kinds
become direct challenges; where children do as their disrespect-
ful parents do; and policemen and other public guardians and
officials appear to the punks to be only spoil sports. Once upon
a time a punk was an inexperienced hand, a beginner, and the
term was temporary, almost probationary. Today the punk is a
juvenile delinquent who hopes to grow up to be a monster.

Actually, relatively little that is corrupt in our society has
any direct connection with advertising. Murder, rape and armed
robbery have never had the benefit of even an exploratory ap-
propriation. No advertising of which I am aware has ever promoted party crashing, purse snatching, shop-lifting, mugging,
tax dodging, cop hating or the juice racket. Sit-ins, lay-downs
and drop-outs are as foreign to promotion through advertising

as mononucleosis and drug addiction. Farm surpluses and the high price of haircuts, doctors' prescriptions, hospital beds and downtown parking all have come to pass without any use of paid space or time.

Advertising has yet to be written to drum up attendance at race riots or church burnings.

There is nothing in the annals of the business that could have served as a model for either the Beatles or Bobby Baker, Billy Sol Estes, Sonny Liston, the Uris brothers, Phyllis Diller or Mae Craig. There has never been a line of advertising to support the arrogance of James Hoffa or Maria Callas, or the tantrums of Melvin Belli or the average U. S. tennis star. The nastiness of Lenny Bruce is entirely his own, while insofar as advertising is concerned neither Henry Cabot Lodge, Gladys Towle Root, Adam Clayton Powell, Governor Wallace or Leo Durocher could be proved to exist . . .

Most of the viewers who fear advertising as an evil force give it too much credit. The medium isn't that good. About all I can do under even the most skillful direction is to exploit a given interest, predilection, disposition, prejudice or bias and bring this to bear on a buying decision. The thing to remember is that the given interest, predilection, etc., usually has to be there first. It is quite true that probing by advertising people sometimes uncovers prejudices not previously known to exist. However, they rarely invent these.

The effect of advertising upon most of us is to help resolve the choice of alternatives that confront us in the normal course of every day. What the hard-working critics forget is that they and only they undertake to look at *all* advertising; the rest of us sort out automatically what we need and pay little attention to what is left. One of the most highly developed functions of the human brain closes it instantly to advertising that is unnecessary or uninteresting, and neither sound nor fury can open it except at the advertiser's risk; he can shout himself from disinterest to disapproval in a single sixty-second commercial.

The power of advertising is greatest when it helps to answer questions. Shall we buy a new car or install a swimming pool? Will the old refrigerator do, and if it will, shall we save for color television or shall we make over the family room? Is this the year for a World's Fair trip, or would a boat mean much more lasting fun? Those are large questions.

And there are many little ones: what kind of shirt, socks, bra, sheets, towels, cold cream, tooth paste, razor blades, frozen foods, canned meats, coffee, soup mix, soap, detergent, facial tissues, floor wax, greeting cards or diet cola should we choose this time? These are the questions advertising helps to answer every day.

Let me go back to cigaret advertising, which I have suggested is a good deal less potent than some critics think. The figures are revealing...

The 2.5 billion cartons of cigarets sold annually in the U. S. are divided between twenty-six advertised brands. The bottom five brands spent as much last year to sell 31.5 million cartons as the number one brand spent to sell 365 million cartons!

Altogether, I think there may be more in advertising to concern an economist than there is to worry a sociologist.

1965

March 25

Typically, the undergraduates [of today] are deadly serious young people. Their feelings are pressing them toward convictions. And one of these concerns advertising.

According to a survey conducted by Louis Harris and Associates and the staff of *Newsweek,* and reported in that magazine for March 22, even organized labor and the Republican Party are viewed with greater confidence by students than advertising and its ugly handmaiden, television ...

The economy of luxury in which we live (and which supports all of our institutions of learning) cannot function without advertising. There is no other way for products and services to be marketed so widely; there is not time enough in anyone's life to make the hundreds of buying comparisons and judgments that we all must make, week after week after week. The choice is endless and so are our selections.

But if confidence in advertising should somehow disappear, then I think much of advertising itself would disappear. Perhaps only retail advertising and the want ad would be left, except for special announcements.

There are those, of course, who say we don't need advertising, or choice; that choice is wasteful. But these are theorists.

And their theories apply to animals (and monks and nuns and eremites who choose to renounce choice). Even the Russians have discovered that choice is the only fuel that fires the economic boilers and keeps them heated. Now the Russians have discovered advertising; they may soon decide that they invented it.

Meanwhile, almost half of those questioned said they had "hardly any" confidence in advertising. Thirty-eight per cent had "only some" confidence. And only sixteen per cent had a "great deal" of confidence.

I wish I could blame the unbelievers, but this is impossible. Too many people who use advertising and too many people who make advertising do this with cynical disregard for any other value than the value of money. For the most part these malefactors are prevented from practicing outright fraud. The blatant lie is banned. But there is a kind of scrupulous dishonesty abroad in advertising, and particularly in television advertising, that could pull the whole house down.

One of these days someone is going to explain and expose the weasel. The weasel is the flaw in the promise that makes it no promise at all, and thus legal.

No matter what the commercials say, it is impossible for all synthetic detergents to cut dishpan grease fastest yet be kindest to your hands; and if Ajax detergent is stronger than dirt (and great for white horses) what of it? What other detergent isn't stronger than dirt? It is impossible for five different analgesics all to work faster, more effectively than any other, and have the least side effect. It is impossible for ten different cigarets all to give you more flavor. And so on and on. And it is also impossible, I think, for advertising of this kind eventually to move sensible people to anything but disillusion and disgust.

As matters stand, a fairly large number of advertisers are successfully playing the public for suckers. But this is a diminishing public. It is diminished by the incessant yammering of dreadful television advertising. You could skip a good deal of foolish copy in print and it rarely provoked anyone who wasn't looking for something to object to. Television advertising is different; it is inescapable and it is powerful; indeed, it is so obtrusive that if ever it gets much worse the *public* could well wash their hands of it, joining the students.

The result then would be that for some period of time, perhaps a generation, maybe longer, most products and most services would be bought on price alone — and mostly at the lowest price.

This would be a heavy penalty for business to pay. But if all products in any given category are advertised as being the best, which can only mean that they are alike and that no choice is necessary, I think we can expect to see the day.

Having deprived television of any chance to shine as an entertainment medium by their insistence on the largest possible enlistment of what Henry L. Mencken used to call the booboise at all hours of the day and night, the spoilers are now grinding out advertising that is as irresponsible and revolting as the most popular programs.

This college generation, which seems bent on revolt, could make a considerable part of advertising a joke and laugh it out of any significance.

Trumped up competitive advertising for identical products is a misuse of advertising by the come-lately and the copy-cat. Advertising should bring news, or be a helpful reminder. When it does anything else it is useless in print and a nuisance and a thief of time on the air.

Altogether, I find it difficult to argue with the campus vote. I just hope that our efforts will continue to qualify as notable exceptions to the current distressing tendencies. Perhaps a few of us, working diligently, can turn the rising tide.

June 18

As anyone knows who remembers the radio program called "Information, Please," John Kieran, sports writer for *The New York Times,* has a remarkable memory . . .

However, Mr. Kieran is not so good on names . . . Kieran didn't like Mr. Hill, whose American Tobacco Company killed "Information, Please," and in his book he refers to the famous tobacco man who proudly bore the name of the father of his country, as George H. Hill! . . .

Another individual whose memory of George Washington Hill is faulty is Mr. Edward L. Bernays, the dean of public relations men, in whose own autobiography Mr. Hill is pictured as sitting in his office glowering beneath a wide-brimmed sombrero. Now, either Bernays never actually saw Hill, who did, indeed, invariably wear a hat in his office; or the New York City publicity agent never has seen a sombrero. George Hill always wore an exceedingly soft, narrow-brimmed hat of a style known as a Knox Crusher.

For some reason all his own, Mr. Hill's Crusher was dented downward four ways from the peak to the ribbon in the style affected by gandy dancers on the Western railroads, on one hand, and President Theodore Roosevelt, on the other; and the ribbon was speckled with trout flies.

The very thought of wearing a Mexican (or Spanish) hat would have put Mr. Hill into one of the high dudgeons that he practiced daily . . .

But it isn't only John Kieran and Edward L. Bernays who disfigure the memory of George Washington Hill.

A recent issue of the Schwerin Research Corporation Bulletin, referring to advertising myths, says "Everyone recalls the story of how Ben Duffy, then president of BBDO, is supposed to have got the Lucky Strike account after a few minutes conversation with Hill. According to one version (which we shall call apocryphal) Duffy landed the account when he muttered the magic incantation 'L.S./M.F.T.' "

Well, there may be people who recall how Ben Duffy is supposed to have got the Lucky Strike account after a few minutes conversation with Hill. But there is one small error in such a recollection. Mr. Duffy never met Mr. Hill. Mr. Hill was the client of Foote, Cone & Belding, which handled the advertising for Lucky Strike cigarets from the day of the agency's founding until after Mr. Hill's death in 1946. It was not until more than a year later, when Foote, Cone & Belding resigned the tobacco company account, that Ben Duffy received the appointment from Vincent Riggio, who succeeded Mr. Hill as president.

As to the "magic incantation," L.S./M.F.T. was the joint inspiration of George W. Hill and Fairfax M. Cone. However, this was strictly a one-horse, one-rabbit collaboration.

"What do you think I am doing here," Mr. Hill asked me as I sat down across the desk from him one wintry afternoon at 111 Fifth Avenue. He was drumming with a small gold-tipped bamboo pencil on the glass top of his dark mahogany desk.

It sounded as if he were tapping out something in Morse Code. And I said so.

"That," he said, "is precisely what I am doing."

"But do you know what it says?" he added.

"No," I said.

"Listen," he said, "Listen hard. L.S.M./F.T. L.S.M./F.T. Lucky Strike Means/fine tobacco. Can't you hear *that* on your radio?"

Of course I could. And all America did for years thereafter.

My contribution was to put the pause after Lucky Strike, instead of Lucky Strike Means/fine tobacco.

This wasn't much. But, at least, my friend Ben Duffy had nothing to do with it; except to inherit it several years later from Vincent Riggio.

August 13

As so often happens, the head-shaking and the fist-pounding at the Spring meetings (the annual meetings) of the American Association of Advertising Agencies and the Association of National Advertisers have resulted in nothing at all.

The 4A's Study on Consumer Judgment of Advertising turned up some numbers which showed that 84% of the advertisements that people are exposed to evoke no response one way or the other, favorable or unfavorable, and the press accounts of the meeting at The Greenbrier were filled with sadness.

Paul Harper, Jr., the president of Needham, Harper & Steers, is reported to have said "What a way to die."

Bill Lewis, chairman of Kenyon & Eckhardt, is supposed to have said, "Any agency president or chairman who doesn't get goose pimples from this evidence of advertising's minimal impact is kidding himself."

Maybe they did say these things, but I doubt that the context is clear. The study wasn't nearly that frightening except to that part of the advertising trade press that feeds on unease.

The ANA study entitled "Management's Role in Effective Advertising" which was planned by certain ANA members to smoke out dissatisfaction with the commission system of agency compensation managed only to come up with the curious suggestion that many advertisers were studying the prevailing system but were doing this without their agencies' knowledge. This, of course, is nonsense. Where, except within the agencies themselves, could anyone study either the operation or the results of *any* agency compensation system?

The effectiveness of specific advertising and the cost to advertisers of agency service are certainly areas for continuing investigation. Most large agencies and most large advertisers study them together as a matter of course. The trouble with the ANA study and the 4A's survey is that both were undertaken with high hopes that failed to materialize in the findings. The 4A's hoped to discover that advertising as an institution is recognized as a highly salient feature of the good American life; and the ANA wanted to take some starch out of the agencies' posture as marketing experts and relegate them entirely to the advertising function, possibly at cut prices.

Just so, the two studies had nothing in common except their lack of important findings, and both advertising and the advertiser-agency relationship are left just where they were, and for several good reasons.

That only 16% of an average day's advertising exposures were categorized as enjoyable, informative, annoying or offensive by a fair sample of the public seems to me anything but alarming. The figures indicate that of the average seventy-six daily exposures to advertising, twelve take, as it were; and of these, four may be categorized as informative, four enjoyable and four annoying or offensive. (The numbers are approximate.)

One of the things this study underscores is that most people are not looking at manufacturers' advertising or listening to manufacturers' advertising as a means of diversion. That they are sometimes entertained briefly, as by some commercials on television, is not surprising; but it is largely irrelevant. Advertising is a means of selling and there is no more to be gained from amusing people, unless somehow this also moves them toward a purchase, than there is from annoying them or offending them.

Nevertheless, if, as the study indicates, the one-third of the day's advertisements categorized as informative really make an impression, I would say this would be an excellent score, particularly if you could multiply it by seven, which is the number of days in a week, or by thirty, which is the average number of days in a month. If the figure is projectable, it multiplies to twenty-eight informative (and presumably, moving) advertisements that get through to a responsive audience in a week and one hundred twelve that are effective during four weeks.

The thing to remember, of course, is that the responsive audience for one product is not necessarily the responsive audience for another. Every product must seek its own interested public. And every advertiser must remember that not even his best prospects are equally interested in his product advertising at all times. A woman who has just bought a vacuum cleaner after carefully shopping the field is not likely to be avidly reading vacuum cleaner advertisements; men are not likely to pay close attention to the advertising of products bought and used primarily by women; and so on.

If 11 per cent of all the advertising to which the average individual is exposed on an average day makes some favorable impression on that individual, remembering how the mixture of advertising changes from day to day, I would think that sensible and timely advertising is pretty effective . . .

November 1

Tall, loose-jointed, relaxed as Fred Astaire, Smith at fifty-seven looks a good deal more like a graying college professor than a typical advertising man.

If this had been written only once, and only about Smith, I suppose I would have thought nothing of it as I read the last lines of the profile in one of the broadcasting trade magazines. The thing that caught me up was the realization that the writer had paid his greatest compliment to an advertising agent: that he didn't even look (for it had been inferred earlier in the piece that he didn't seem to act, either) like the advertising prototype!

Thinking about this I am sure now that I have read at least a dozen times about advertising men who, presumably fortunately, looked anything but the part.

This I find interesting, because search as I have I can find no picture to show nor printed words to describe what it is that an advertising man is *supposed* to look like. A good many years ago he was drawn into a gray flannel suit, with a double martini as the principal prop in the picture. But I'm sure this doesn't apply any more. I don't know a man in our business who could appear composed in public in flannel of any color . . .

Advertising men, quite despite the novelists and the columnists, are generally a fairly frugal, as well as sober, lot. They are a little like professional baseball players who, whatever they might like to do with their money, must save it against the day when their arms and their legs are worn out and they must find some other kind of business to help them make a living. Advertising people wear out, too, through stress and strain and crises that are not usually of their own making but, inevitably, become theirs to work out of.

Advertising men are for the most part not only sensitive but also sensible. They sense the gradual erosion of interest and the energy and devotion that are necessary for top-flight performance and most of them save thoughtfully against the time when they must give way to fast-balling youth.

There are remarkably few poor retired advertising men. If some of them look like graying college professors, it is perhaps only because they would have been good at that, too.

November 17

The notion that the public is insensitive when its leg is pulled is current only among eggheads, longhairs, highbrows and the great unwashed who infest the universities.

Advertising's present folly results from the mistaken idea that it has something to gain from an unholy alliance with show business. This, of course, is a development that must be blamed on broadcasting. However, the emergence of radio and television as our principal means of entertainment should have nothing to do with advertising, except as they may carry it.

Advertising is selling and selling is a serious business. There is no place in it for knights on armored horses chasing dirt, tornados in kitchen sinks washing dishes, clothes so clean that they may safely be viewed only through smoked glasses, blacked eyes based on cigaret brand loyalty, etc.

Advertising couldn't possibly have a worse model than the theatre, where the standard performance in the industry is failure. As I said at the Plaza, there is only one success in every thirty legitimate attempts to write a song or a play or a movie, even a television show. And this is not nearly a good enough percentage for any other business.

What I didn't know when I was talking was that of the three new plays that opened in New York the previous week, one lasted through eight performances, one lasted through four showings, and the third expired after a single outing.

That two of the shows were billed as hilarious comedies underscores the lesson for advertisers, who are doing about equally badly with their own amateur theatricals in television and in print.

My favorite recent headline in a magazine advertisement was "How would you like an acid bath?", a question asked by a steel fabricator.

The only sensible answer I could think of was "How would *you* like a punch in the nose?"

Carmel, Calif., December 7

Perhaps a psychiatrist could tell me precisely why my recurring dreams are dreams of frustration. However, I am not entirely sure that I want to know, for the relief I experience upon waking from these dreams amounts almost to jubilation, and I have often tried to recapture them in a kind of half sleep just for the thrill of waking up.

It is a little bit like re-reading terribly unhappy passages in a book that you know is going to work out all right in the end ...

[One of three] noteworthy experiences with dreams was with a continuing one that I managed somehow to prolong into three chapters or episodes in the fall of 1958.

This has to do with our solicitation of the Edsel advertising account. It began with a recreation of our original presentation in the conference room next to Larry Doyle's office in the temporary headquarters of the new division at Dearborn, Michigan, in November of 1957.

My dilemma was that although I knew we had rehearsed the presentation the previous day at the Book-Cadillac Hotel in Detroit, I couldn't recognize any of my colleagues. They could have been and, indeed, were complete strangers.

The second night the dream progressed to the point where I recognized my associates all right, but I couldn't, for the life of me, remember their names. Every time I finally got one he changed to somebody else.

The third night was the night of the great switch. We were making our presentation not to Dick Krafve, Larry Doyle and Bob Copeland of Ford, but to Leo Burnett and a jury of Burnett people including Bill Young, Strother Cary and Jim Weber, and also, inexplicably under the circumstances, to Marion Harper of McCann-Erickson.

However, it was none of these gentlemen but, instead, America's sweetheart, Mary Pickford, who awarded us the account.

It wasn't until long after the real award had actually been

made to us by Messrs. Krafve, Doyle and Copeland that I came to wish Miss Pickford had made it to Burnett.

December 15

Foote, Cone & Belding, Chicago, is the second largest advertising agency in town, second to Burnett, but this is something you could never tell most Chicago cab drivers.

Say "155 East Superior Street" and three out of five drivers will reply "Foote, Cone & Belding?" . . .

There will be no more such surprises, for the chapter is about to close on the building that has served us so well for so long. When we get into a cab next week and thereafter and say "Equitable Building, please," or "401 North Michigan Avenue," we could be going to call on the Harvester people, or someone in the Equitable itself, or even to work at Needham, Harper & Steers or Time, Inc., or the McCall Corporation, and I must confess that this makes me a little sad.

Not that I don't like our new offices. I like them very much. I think they are exquisitely planned and beautifully executed, on a magnificent site, and they give us the additional space we so desperately have come to need. Who would have dreamed, five years ago, for example, that we were going to require an electronic computer room three times the size of our auditorium?

I am only sad because the bronze letters that marked our own building, which was the only such building in Chicago, stood for the agency's individuality. Not only were we different in many ways from any other advertising company, but we looked it, and we looked it with dignity and what I think has been reasonable and understandable pride . . .

1966

February 2

One of the continuing troubles with the business we are in is that anyone who has the price can practice it. The field is wide open. Rascality aside, there are no rules. The sky is the limit. The hell with Esther Peterson; also the Federal Trade Commission, the Federal Drug Administration and the Better Business Bureaus. None of these has anything to do with taste.

One has only to watch television on any night to know how

low it has sunk. It is doubtful if there is a single script in a month's production of this year's situation comedies that could make it, all fleshed out, as a short story in *Good Housekeeping* magazine . . .

Nor are the commercials in television any better. Substance has given way to utter foolishness that is redeemed not at all by magnificent mechanical and artistic production.

The automobile people are in the van, and Chevrolet has set some kind of record with a double spread in *Life* magazine, which undertakes to explain why an Impala convertible was shown on the Bonanza program perched on the thin top of Castle Rock, some thousand feet or so above the desert at Moab, Utah.

The advertisement explains, somewhat dubiously I am afraid, that this symbolizes "an attitude, summed up in these words 'The Chevrolet Way'." But the explanation fails to reveal that the Chevrolet in question, without a motor, was lifted by helicopter to the top of the stone column where a second helicopter then dropped the petrified live model into the front seat.

This, according to the Chevrolet advertisement in *Life,* is "on the road performance."

Thus does advertising in television seek to entertain rather than to tell viewers something that may be useful, or even important, to know. The fault, of course, is the advertisers' and the agents' together. Now that they have been booted out of programming by the moguls, they have turned to the commercials for their kicks.

(The Chevrolet advertisement in question was repeated in 1973 because, it said, so many people had asked how it was made.

(Thus the advertisement rather than the product took the spotlight. This is the danger of what I can only call over-creativity. We see it again and again in attempts to copy highly successful television commercials like those for Gillette's Right Guard deodorant and Miles Laboratories' Alka-Seltzer, where the products play a leading role in the sixty-second dramas.

(How difficult this is is underscored by the fact that not even Gillette and Miles can copy their own successes without a certain number of failures—almost always due to over-reaching.)

February 24

One of the easiest things to do in business is to fire an advertising agency.

This is something I have never done. But I have been on the receiving end a number of times. For various reasons. Some good and some not so good.

Once our company was dismissed because one of its managers mailed some harsh political judgments to a California newspaper in an agency envelope. It was felt that he was trying to influence the press; and that he was I have no doubt.

Later on we were fired by the client who inspired the unfortunate mailing. Apparently we hadn't done anything foolish for him lately.

Another client walked us off a plank because one of our managers wouldn't quit his job and team up with the client in the agency business. This was one that we stood to lose either way.

Sometimes the timing of a dismissal is almost unbelievable.

Several years ago we were discharged by a large advertiser only a few weeks after his company had done away with its own advertising department and delegated its authority as well as its duties to the agency.

No reason was ever given for our termination. We were generously paid off. But still there was no explanation for the company's abrupt action.

Usually agencies and their clients who come to a parting of the ways do so because of a slow deterioration in their regard for each other. However, management changes account for a good many terminations, too; new managements that are not the result of long-time planned advancements tend to look upon inheriting an agency as somehow impinging on their personal prerogatives. We have lost more accounts for this reason than for any other.

We also lost one because a man blamed us for a costly mistake that was really his own. Several years later the man was expelled from his golf club for fabricating his score in a tournament. What this had to do with our reappointment by his employer, I do not know, but this occurred shortly afterward.

Conflict of interest and security have recently been given as the reason for several agency changes, and these have been the subject of a number of articles and editorials in the advertising trade press. Undoubtedly there is some risk in almost every confidential business operation; somebody may spill the beans, accidentally or on purpose. What nobody has pointed out to my knowledge is that banks are engaged every day in confidential undertakings for competitive companies; also, the constant movement of key employees through the whole business system makes security very hard to maintain without putting it up to the advertising agencies.

As far as I know there has never been a leak out of one of the leading agencies. This would be unthinkable from the principals and this is what all the people with classified information hope to be.

Incidentally, I discovered long ago that if one of our clients wants to know something about a competitor he can usually find out through the simple expedient of calling the competitor on the telephone and asking him for the information.

The most elaborate security system in industry operates in Detroit. Yet every year when the new cars are introduced it takes months to learn to tell them apart. Everyone knows almost precisely what everyone else is going to do and the copying is completed long before the advertising agencies have their first look at the models.

Firing an agency must be a little bit like firing a doctor. You rarely tell the old doctor why you have left him. Maybe you don't actually know. Maybe you've heard something about another doctor, somebody who has developed a fascinating treatment for something you've decided may be bothering you. Your old doctor doesn't know about this; you didn't either until your friend mentioned it to you or you read about it under Medicine in *Time* magazine.

So off you go to a new man, avoiding your old doctor on the street or at parties, and easing your conscience by telling anyone who will listen what a great fellow he is.

This is the way people talk about advertising agencies, too; after they secretly call in, or let in, some new people.

The only thing wrong with this is the hypocrisy that goes along with it. The reluctance with which most advertisers admit to their agencies that changes are impending even when these are completely planned and dated, can only be accounted for on the basis that the reasons for the change are not very good ones.

Somebody has been sold something.

But let me come back to the analogy with the doctor-patient relationship. Let's say the agency in question hasn't been doing a thoroughly satisfactory job; something is wrong, somewhere, somehow. The easiest thing in the world is to fire them. The trouble is, this may be the worst thing to do.

A friend of mine had a very unsuccessful cataract operation; in fact it was a total failure. But when it came to a second operation, to repair the damage, he went resolutely back to the doctor who had failed him. "Who knows more about my case?" he reasoned. "Who else would know so well why the first operation did not succeed? Who has so much at stake in success this time?"

The answers to all these questions were the same. The operation was performed by the original surgeon, and it was a complete success.

If more business men took the same very sensible attitude toward advertising agencies, and worked out their problems with them instead of transferring these, this would be a happier business for everyone concerned.

Meanwhile, we gain just as we suffer from changes in the advertiser's assignments, and I don't suppose I would be thinking about this today were it not for the fact that the daily press has taken to reporting these with a relish that once was reserved for murder and rape.

A man I hadn't seen for a year stopped me on the street the other day and said, "I see you got sacked by Armour."

"No," I said, "it was General Foods."

"Well," he said, "I knew it was somebody."

The man was a doctor.

May 3

There is one thing about the House of Seagram that makes me wonder.

It seems to take them forever and a day to learn anything, and when one branch does learn something it is apparently maintained as a closely guarded secret from all the other branches of the family.

In the case of Calvert's "soft" whiskey, Seagram tells us that "this isn't something we cooked up overnight. Distillers have tried to make soft whiskey for years. Even we flopped in 22,000 experiments before we had it."

The new taste of Four Roses wasn't anything Seagram came up with overnight either.

"Far from it," they say.

"For one thing, we had a cupboard full of 1,500 different whiskies to work with. And before we found just the right combination (some 50 different tasting whiskies and grain neutral spirits in all) a lot of new gray hairs had appeared on the scene."

Clearly these things took time and cost money. But they were as nothing compared to the effort and the years during which the secrets of Scotch whiskey eluded what were Seagram's evidently not-too-bright researchers.

In developing 100 Pipers, says Seagram in its newest advertising campaign, "we spent about 10 years searching out Scotland's greatest whiskies.

"Then another 10 or so finding the right combination.

"Finally, after exhaustive investigation we got our Scotch."

The quotes are precise. From current periodicals. In what is probably the strangest case of fumbling and bumbling on record by any large American company.

I think if I had anything to do with Seagrams I would get myself some new boys.

Or maybe, a new advertising agency.

Incidentally, Seagram says it got the idea of combining great Scotch whiskies from the 1933 All-Star baseball team of the American League.

On the record this may be so. Still it seems incredible that nobody at Seagram was aware that George Ballantine & Son of Dunbarton, Scotland, had been purveying the same thing since 1827. This is printed right on the Ballantine label.

As I said, Seagram has me wondering.

May 10

There is nothing new about idiocy in advertising. It is as old as fraud.

Like fraud it turns up in a new disguise every year. Just now we are treated to such lunacies as the girl who won't without her green stripe, Axelrod, round tires, soft whiskey, goof-proof cocktails, and tigers, tigers everywhere.

The girl who won't without her green stripe is Tiffany Eubank, a blond who presently appears in print in a matador's suit

in behalf of Usher's Green Stripe Scotch whiskey. Since there is
no explanation, one must assume that pretty Tiffany gets her
urge for adventure from the bottle, and that this is good.

Of course, I know better. You can't promise any benefit at
all from wine or beer or spirits. The Alcohol Tax Unit of the
U. S. Treasury Department won't let you. Still, Tiffany Eubank
has survived a free fall from an airplane, as well as the perils
of the bull ring; and if hers isn't Dutch courage, what is it?

Axelrod is less confusing, but no less absurd. Axelrod is a
long-eared, sad-eyed basset hound. His face is a map of concern to remind you that Flying A service station attendants
really worry about your car. I, for one, would rather see the
attendants, and at $50,000 per page in *Life* magazine, Axelrod
would seem to be something other than a bargain.

Next we have round tires, which are the proposition upon
which the makers of Atlas Polycrons challenge Goodyear,
Goodrich, U. S. Royal, etc., and I find it hard to believe that
any of the millions of riders on the latter can be convinced that
they are bounding around on square or even elliptical treads.
When Atlas says that we should insist on round tires, I would
assume that everyone does, and turn to another station.

In the matter of soft whiskey, I am afraid there is no such
thing; and the argument that is undertaken to support this
Calvert Extra story is almost classic double talk.

"A lady can even drink soft whiskey straight," it goes,
"without batting an eyelash. Soft whiskey swallows nice and
easy, treating her ever so tenderly.

"But don't get the wrong idea. Soft whiskey is no softie.
It's 86 proof. And does exactly what any 86 proof does. It just
does it softer.

"Now, about the softening process. All we can tell you is,
some Calvert Extra is distilled in small batches instead of huge
ones. Forgive our being so close mouthed. But we fell flat on
our faces in year after year of experiments before we found the
formula."

This formula, I dare say, was really discovered, perfected
and approved in an advertising conference and the dipsy doodle
about treating the lady tenderly is pure advertising invention.

Goof-proof cocktails (also Calvert's) may prove to have a
popular appeal, but I have an idea that the handy alliteration is
unfortunate.

To begin with, ready-mixed cocktails are not generally purchased by sophisticates. Knowledgeable people *like* to make cocktails; they are proud of their artistry. And if they are to be won over to the bottled variety they are probably going to have to have a little more enticing reason than goof-proof, which is strictly an appeal to a duffer. On the other hand, the cocktail (except for the Manhattan and the whiskey sour) requires an educated taste and I doubt if giving it the bus driver's designation is going to put it over with the McGimpers.

The tigers are another matter. They all came out of a successful campaign for Oklahoma gasoline that was dropped some years ago when Humble bought the Oklahoma Oil Company and put its money behind the Enco label. After a suitable period of interment, Barbara Feldon brought the tiger back to help her with the Top Brass hair paste commercials on television, after which a whole parade of manufacturers of tires, automobiles, textiles, and whatnot, followed suit. Now even Enco has returned to its old sponsorship.

Alas, however, the tiger that used to go into your gas tank, which made a kind of exaggerated sense, now sits in the front seat with you—which doesn't make any sense at all.

Ever since John Kennedy defined advertising as salesmanship in print, and Claude Hopkins implemented that definition with the insistence that salesmanship in print required a reason why it was in the prospective customer's best selfish interest to accept the advertiser's promise, it has been the first rule of advertising that its promise should immediately be clear.

If it isn't, nothing else matters.

The message may be important, but if it isn't clear very few people are going to dig out that fact. There is simply no accounting for Tiffany Eubank or Axelrod, and it is doubtful if anyone has tried.

Nevertheless, this foolishness goes on and on.

*

Renault headlines "Our customers are dissatisfied." Volvo suggests that "If you'd like a good used Volkswagen see your Volvo dealer." Fiat asks whether "The second best shape in Italy (shown alongside a busty girl) is quite proper for a family man?"

Nor are the above the only admirers of the off-beat and the obscure.

Ac'cent, the sodium glutamate, offers you "25 cents to take a bugle lesson," which is the reward for tracing the bugle on an Ac'cent package. Hudson paper towels offer printed borders that "feed your soul." Polaroid asks you "to explain to your wife why you went and bought the most expensive color pack camera there is, when you could have gotten one that makes pictures just as good and just as fast for less than half the price, big shot."

Mercury tells you that "Ben Franklin discovered the Mercury." Only this is a modern Ben Franklin, of Wantagh, New York. Quaker Oats insists that "on a c-c-c-cold morning, Mama, a kid needs a little stove in his tummy." And good old Chiquita Banana, taking a cue from Tareyton's black-eyes and the hat-eaters of the ludicrous Lucky Strike advertising, asks you to "look for the seal on the peel and wear it in good health" (like the dunce in the picture that follows).

Just why anyone should want to read about an automobile whose customers are dissatisfied, or buy a Volkswagen from the Volvo dealer is beyond my imagination. Prospects for bugle lessons must surely be one of the world's tiniest minorities. I don't know whether Polaroid is trying to sell me a high-priced Polaroid or a low-priced Polaroid; moreover, I don't like being called "big shot" by a smart aleck copywriter.

And I'll be damned if I think a Chiquita Banana label is any kind of decoration for anyone's forehead.

*

Advertising is not a game to be played. It is a substitute, and only a fairly satisfactory substitute, for personal, face-to-face selling. It is something you do when you can't go see someone. Thus it needs, above all, clarity. For once you are embarked on an advertisement, in any medium, there is no turning back to begin again if someone doesn't understand you.

The best way I know to be sure that we are on the right track is to make our advertising proposition out loud, as if to a friend, before putting it down on paper. If we can't speak the opening sentence of a commercial on television or radio, or the headline of a printed advertisement, without adding "I mean" and explaining what it is that we really do mean, we should discard it. It has to be sayable and it has to be sensible to be of any use. If it isn't, nothing can save the advertisement.

If you don't believe me, I suggest you try telling a friend about the Dodge revolution.

June 21

It is the second essential of a good advertisement that the proposition it makes shall be important.

In other words, what is clear must also be of some consequence. It must make a reasonable appeal to the self-interest of its logical prospects. It must promise a worthwhile benefit.

Television advertising, which is reeling from the unexpected kudos heaped upon it by a number of critics who have suggested that today's commercials are more entertaining than most of the programs they interrupt, frequently makes no sense at all. For even the most lavish and imaginative production is of no value if it fails to make a promise that is clear and attractive.

Chevrolet was one of the first of the big-time advertisers to succumb to the virus of over-production. Perching cars on offshore rocks sprayed with sea spray or floating them in the canals of Venice is in elaborate defiance of all reason.

Plymouth has followed suit. A current color commercial for Plymouth's Fury concerns itself with a native wedding on a South Sea atoll — after which the delirious bride and groom bounce off through the tropic overgrowth to give the flame red Fury seven brief, blurred seconds in the sequence.

It may be that both the Plymouth and the Chevrolet advertising is everything the bemused critics look for as evidence of blossoming television art and imagery. Goodness knows it *is* superior artistically to most of the programs it punctuates. But it isn't advertising. And insofar as advertising helps sell automobiles, which probably isn't very far except in the case of Volkswagen where superb copy and art made the little bugs legitimate, it seems to have fallen down badly in comparison with Ford's advertising of Ford features.

Ford sales are up. Chevrolet and Plymouth sales are down. And Plymouth has changed advertising agencies.

But the virus will be found there, too.

A masterpiece of tomfoolery from Plymouth's new agency appeared in print last week under the headline "Peel our new avocado," which turns out to be the green border color of a new Gala paper towel. Imaginative? Yes. Clear and important? No.

This is advertising for that surely small group of people who get their kicks out of trying to figure out what it is the copywriters are being so mysterious about.

Some of these mysteries are done in pictures and some with words. A seven-column newspaper advertisement for Martin's V.V.O. Scotch Whisky contains the single word "Yes" over a picture of a girl in a peasant blouse who holds a small cocktail glass filled with what is presumably Martin's V.V.O. But Yes what? The advertisement gives no clue.

Another strange newspaper advertisement, and one from a very good agency, has no formal headline at all, but, instead, the following discourse:

"Mark Mullen has business in Los Angeles. He's attending a two-day seminar on 'The Southeast Asian Export Outlook.'

"Mark's wife and daughter have business in Los Angeles, too. But they won't be attending the two-day seminar on 'The Southeast Asian Export Outlook.' (In fact they'll be lucky if they see all of Disneyland in two days.)"

Only after all this is it disclosed that the family pictured in the advertisement is "Flying on United Airlines Family Plan, with one-third off coach fare for Mrs. Mullen. Two-thirds off for Mark's daughter." This is the proposition, and a pretty attractive one, too, buried eighty-one words deep in the meandering text.

This can't be right. Advertising has to work much faster. It has to get to the important proposition at once. And again, of course, this has to be truly important.

An advertisement in last week's *Time* magazine calls Old Thompson American whiskey the quiet blend. There is also the Corina Baron—a quiet cigar. And I would ask you what in the world a quiet whiskey or a quiet cigar can possibly be. Neither Old Thompson nor old Corina undertakes to tell.

Another remarkable page in *Time* last week claimed that "Not one of the world's 17 great lovers is fat."

The one photographed (identified only as #9) is sailing, the advertisement says, "to Portofino with Claudine, Ingrid and Marie-Louise" who are shown in their bikinis on the deck of the lover's boat. "He runs a taut ship, and sports a trim build. And like many another great lover, he relies on Metrecal," it says.

And so Metrecal, in extremely bad taste, dumps its important dietetic promise, and wraps up an untidy idea in a dubious charade.

But all is not wrong with advertising, even in television.

The Goodyear tire commercials on the U. S. Open Golf Championship broadcasts from San Francisco proved once again how durable is an important proposition. These were new variations on the appeal to thoughtful men that has sparked Goodyear Life Guard tire advertising for several years. "When there is no man around, Goodyear should be," say the commercials. And they prove this by showing how these Goodyear tires have an inner tire that holds fast when the outer casing is punctured, making it unnecessary for a woman driver ever to change a tire on the road.

This is advertising that doesn't fool around.

Nor does any thoughtful advertising person dare. Research tells us that the average citizen in the U. S. is exposed to more than 1,500 advertisements each day. Other research finds that fewer than ten of these 1,500 attempts to attract his attention are successful. If these figures are anywhere near right, we can't afford to fool around, in any medium.

July 6

I trust that no recent memo of mine has conveyed the idea that I find something wrong with imagination in advertising.

The fact is, I find advertising that is not imaginative almost the dullest stuff I can think of. What I object to is foolishness in advertising: such as a woman rushing across a lawn into the face of a television camera and suddenly disappearing from view to act out the name Open Pit barbecue sauce.

This is what I have referred to before as an advertising charade. It makes no promise. It has no significance. It tells nothing whatever about the product. On the other hand, Kraft barbecue sauce (which promises to simmer real cook-out flavor right into the meat) goes merrily along, increasing its sales lead over Open Pit.

I hold that there is no luck whatever about the leading position of so many products advertised by Foote, Cone & Belding.

Clairol and Contac, Dial and Dole, Sunkist and Hallmark, Hammond and the ten leading products of Johnson and Kraft and Kimberly-Clark, all are advertised with considerable imagination.

They just don't get out of hand. There are no black eyes, no hat eating, no tongue in cheek, no double talk. The sneeze that wrecks the room in the man-size Kleenex commercial is a great piece of comedy (it probably repeats as well as any commercial ever shown on television) but it is only humorous to make a point. A loud sneeze has always been mirthfully greeted. This one provokes a kind of pictorial gesundheit, which is a far, far cry from the wash so white that it blinds its beholder.

Paper-Mate pens, Sara Lee cakes, Sunbeam electric tooth brushes and Zenith television instruments are some other leaders in our list that are represented by advertising that talks the way people talk about things people want to hear about.

This didn't rule out the piggyback refill for Paper-Mate, or writing through butter to prove that Paper-Mate pens do not skip. It didn't rule out peeling the orange in one piece for Sunbeam electric knives. Or Sara Lee's talking cakes, on radio. Or parachuting a working Zenith television set out of an airplane to prove its indestructibility.

The point is that each of these things makes a point. And the right public gets it.

That is what the sales figures show.

July 27

It is another of the essentials of good advertising that the clear, important proposition must also present a personal appeal.

When it doesn't, when it is impersonal, or when the appeal is misdirected, then the advertising is futile. This is one of the great difficulties with today's stand-up comic style of television commercials. The stand-up comic is invariably the hero of the tales he tells; but he is a hero in reverse. He is the goat-hero in an impossible situation.

He is the sufferer.

He is the poor sap.

In advertising, he can't make up his mind whether to offer a lady a cigar (a Tiparillo).

Or, if the goat-hero turns out to be a woman, she may not be able to tell you what cranberry juice tastes like, and stammers to a complete stall in 58 seconds. (The latest from Ocean Spray.)

A good deal of print advertising is similarly stalled.

It isn't clear. It isn't important. And it is impossible to discover, even if one studies it, who it is aimed at. In her most recent outing Tiffany Eubank, who won't without her Green Stripe, appears in fencing costume ready to do battle. But with whom?

Effective advertising always takes a sharp aim.

There has been very little advertising in recent years more consistently ugly than Anacin advertising. But its aim has been perfect. It has always been pointed at sufferers from headache. Maybe it pained everyone else, but it promised prompt and lasting relief to the only television viewers who mattered.

Generally speaking, I suppose the proprietary people, who deal with the most unpleasant subjects, and the food advertisers who dish up the most attractive ones, make the most direct, personal approach.

For one thing, they know precisely who they want to talk to. And I think it is a fact that almost every drug advertisement and almost every food advertisement that you will see this year could be addressed to a single person. It will be that personal.

On the other hand, most advertising of cigarets, soap, detergents, whiskey, beer, automobiles, motorcycles, or whatever, is aimed at no one in particular. Also, it is broadcast to a world that could hardly care less about any given product at any given moment.

What advertising can do, by being clear and sensible and important and properly directed in terms of what it depicts and to whom it makes its promises, is build up a mental commitment to act favorably at an appropriate time. This being the case, advertising should make its propositions in terms of individual wants or needs, to be filled as a responsibility of the advertiser in dealing with sensible people.

There is nothing anywhere more serious than a woman in a supermarket or a department store holding tight to her purse. To believe that her head is awhirl with the absurdities of advertising has to be wrong. The lady can only be interested in proposals that fit her personal notions of need.

And there is rarely anything quixotic about these.

(Here I think it is necessary to repeat that personal health and beauty products are items whose advertising may be effective at the same time that it transcends all reason. Its promise

is confidential and so are the results of the various applications and ingestions.)

August 15

If it is true, as I believe it is, that good advertising is always as personal in its approach as a conversation between two people, it is also true that good advertising makes the personality of the advertiser an attractive part of the advertising promise.

The fact of the matter is that a promise is only as good as its maker.

In some cases in advertising today the mere name of the advertiser is all the guarantee that is required to make his promise immediately iron clad.

The name Johnson on a wax or other household product is a prime example. There is no doubt about any new product that is introduced under its famous banner.

Sometimes, when widely accepted products are not always associated with manufacturers by their trade names, these good names achieve the same result. New products by the makers of Kleenex and Kotex are guaranteed by that association. And the successful introduction of Dial deodorant in test markets is surely attributable to the well-kept promise of Dial soap.

Let me urge you when you look at the advertising of our client companies and their services and their brands to consider how carefully their promises are made. They are rarely overstated; rarely out of character. But if they are overstated they must be out of character. And someone has made a serious mistake.

Like the single bad apple that causes a barrel full of apples to spoil, a single misleading advertisement or one that is out of character may spoil the image of a good name for an incalculable number of people for a long period of time.

Usually, when the mistake is overstatement, it is the result of perfectly honest enthusiasm. When an advertisement is out of character, this generally comes from too great an attempt to be different simply for the sake of variety.

Freshness is something else again.

I don't suppose there are any better examples of continuous freshness in advertising than in the magazine and television advertising of Miss Clairol and Dial deodorant soap. The promise never changes because the products and their purposes never change except for those constant improvements that their makers incorporate as a matter of course and as a matter of keeping their word.

The only changes in the advertising of these two long-time leaders is in the words and pictures that illustrate their continuing promises. Even so, *Does she or doesn't she? Hair color so natural only her hairdresser knows for sure,* and *Aren't you glad you use Dial soap! Don't you wish everybody did?* stand up year after year against millions of dollars arrayed against these propositions.

I cite them here because they are the largest of all our campaigns. Most of our smaller ones are no less consistent. Therein, I think, lies the secret of the very large number of products we work on that stand in undisputed first place.

However, the secret has another part.

The consistence of this advertising is honed on hundreds of attempts to do better. Out of these come the freshness, the little touches that work their way into succeeding campaigns to keep the basic promises alive, and the advertising in character.

There must be no confusion.

It is only our regard for a manufacturer or his product as this is conveyed in advertising that can substitute successfully for the personal solicitation of orders that in our day and age is impossible.

September 15

That advertising is passing through one of its most distressing periods can only be doubted if one believes that we may be stuck in it indefinitely.

If the economy is unable to right itself and we blithely travel the road marked *Inflation,* I imagine that a good deal of advertising will continue to be giddy and irresponsible, too.

Right up to the day of reckoning.

This is the easy way. It appeals to the people who think advertising is a game in which the fundamentals are old-fashioned and not nearly as important as the latest wrinkles, and the wilder the better.

Just now some of the stuff that is coming out of Madison Avenue with loud cheers from the bleachers is almost beyond comprehension—except to the bleacherites. The Braniff Airlines advertising is probably the best example, or the worst, depending upon how you view the scene. It makes me shudder.

A recent Braniff newspaper page called attention to "Another great moment in aviation history" which turns out to be the substitution of china cups for plastic cups in Braniff's coach section. This is spendthrift and lunatic advertising.

Perhaps the worst thing about it is that it is contagious.

Current United Air Lines advertisements, made in Chicago, are garnished with blurbs which emanate from the silhouette of a plane and offer up such goodies as "I always drink Chateaubriand", or "California is full of wild life. Mostly in L. A."

I don't say that such stuff isn't fun (which most airlines advertising for some unaccountable reason tries to be). I won't even say that none of it ever tickles me; I kind of like the fellow who drinks Chateaubriand—at least he's not the phony professional traveler who *always* flies American.

Nevertheless, I have to insist that it isn't advertising.

There are only two wacky patterns that are worse.

The first of these is the advertising that bases its promise on a double entendre. Calvert started this in its campaign for what it called soft whiskey. And of course you know Tiffany Eubank, who won't without her Green Stripe. Now we have a slinky girl in a new Catto (Scotch) campaign who never says "no to Catto".

This kind of thing will probably run a short course. Somebody will venture a little too far down the Primrose Path and the Path will be fenced off. Anyway, there may be an even worse pattern around. It is called exaggerated graphics, and it infests television. It is the White Knight of Ajax who is stronger than dirt. It is Wanda Witch who appears out of nowhere for Hidden Magic hair spray. And now, in the current issue of *McCall's,* it has got into print, where Mary Mild comes floating through the air to say of a woman who is dividing a sack of popcorn with a sheepishly grinning swain, "Her Charlie's a regular Romeo since Ivory Liquid helped her hands look young again."

My respect for Procter & Gamble is great. But this kind of thing is tempting fate.

Not because I say so. I've said it before to no avail.

But there is a foreboding statistic. Only 16% of teen-agers reported in a comprehensive survey of youth in *Look* magazine (September 20) finds advertising "believable".

Says *Look,* "They are skeptical. Forty-one per cent say the Beatles, Madison Avenue and 'the guy out to get a fast buck' set teen-agers' fads. A sixteen-year old boy protests, 'We are brainwashed by the manufacturers'. Television is singled out for abuse. Bucky Frank, 17, of Denver, Colorado, huffs, 'Some TV ads must be directed at morons' ".

I don't think this last is quite true. But the result may be the same. The rush to copy any unusual advertising device leads to all kinds of excesses. The imitations of the White Knight are only one example. The use of large type in place of real news in printed advertising is another.

Of course advertising should be interesting. But it should also stick to business.

October 11

This is about a number of things.

For one, the contention that I first voiced several years ago, that the television networks haven't the remotest idea what the public really wants in entertainment, now is pretty well borne out.

The staggering failure of most of this season's new shows is shared almost equally by the three networks, but the worst flops must be credited to CBS, which has long been the most arrogant and arbitrary and, by all odds, the most financially successful of the broadcasters.

There isn't any question but what CBS has led the pack in the documentary field, but this is a very small one, and the efforts of any network (except to make money) must be judged by its standards in entertainment. For years CBS has gotten by on the slick formula that is represented by the various Lucy shows, Andy Griffith and, say, Gomer Pyle, which is varied only to the extent that Beverly Hillbillies, Petticoat Junction and Green Acres are even more ridiculous; the lines are almost carbon copies and the stupid laugh tracks are identical.

Perhaps the pinnacle of fatuity was reached last month when CBS rescheduled the Garry Moore Show, with Durward Kirby; Sylvester L. Weaver, executive producer. Pat Weaver, when he was president of NBC, joined with Joyce Hall to introduce the Hallmark Hall of Fame, and it is hard to believe that the same man could have committed this hour-long offense whose chief feature was the ineffable Kirby centerstage in his shirttails and baby-blue shorts, grinning and giggling as if the comedy was just too much for him.

CBS should have been mightily ashamed. And perhaps they were, for the program now has been cancelled.

However, the failure of the networks has resulted in an unexpected victory for the viewers. There is now an old moving picture on one station or another in almost every nighttime period, and it is possible to watch a good deal of television without ever becoming involved in the networks' feeble undertakings.

Unfortunately, the commercials are becoming more and more theatrical and more and more obscure, but that is another matter.

*

The third thing that I want to say something about today is the non-stop coverage of the advertising business that has become a feature of large city newspapers and last week burst into the newsweekly field with a nine column story about the Manhattan advertising agency of Wells, Rich, Greene which came out of Jack Tinker's group at Interpublic (with one of Tinker's prize accounts, Braniff) and from whom the following is a fair example:

> Braniff flies to
> Houston
> so often you'd
> think we enjoyed it.

I can only conclude that if Braniff doesn't enjoy flying to Houston, one should choose an airline that at least pretends to.

But my argument isn't so much with pretty Mary Wells. It is more with the press that makes so much of this foolishness, and where the most absurd exercise at the moment is the speculation about a new campaign for Hertz in which the astonishing inside information is whispered that Hertz will no longer "put you in the driver's seat."

Avis, it would appear, has scared them right out of the best thing they had going. But I question whether this is news.

Incidentally, Hertz's new look extends to the remodeling of the old plain, readable Hertz logotype into a design (by Lippincott & Margulies) that is almost illegible.

This, too, has been carefully leaked to the avid press.

Leaked and lapped up.

(Returning to television programming, it is an unhappy fact that until CBS imported "All In the Family" from England and the BBC, in 1971, the standard U. S. fare of repetitive situation comedy and equally uninspired crime shows had remained virtually unchanged for a dozen years. The crime shows had gotten bloodier and the so-called comedies more outlandish and more suggestive. And then there came the talk shows, where a troupe of old- and very young-timers made the rounds of these cheapies, exploiting their talents and their charms, hoping to catch some producer's eye and make it big.

(The only significant change is the replacing of more and more of the comedy and crime programs with movies, both old and new, some of which are pushing crime to new depths of depravity.

(Soon, one may hope, the mine will be exhausted, and in prospecting for substitutes the television moguls will give imagination a chance.)

October 27

The largest editorial headlines in this week's *Life* (October 28) are set in 60 pt. type, in which the capital letters are one-half inch high, the lower case letters half that height.

Some of these headlines are set in Roman faces, some in italics. Some letters have serifs, some are sans-serif.

All are readable.

But like so many commercials on television that are louder than the voices in the programs that carry them, the headlines in a large number of advertisements in this magazine fairly jump off its pages.

Incredible, shouts Smith-Corona in 144 pt. caps and lower case, almost three times the size of the magazine's largest story title.

American Motors calls attention to *NOW CARS* in Gothic caps that are even larger, and in three colors.

Not how much But how good is the 144 pt. headline that compares a string of pearls with a General Dual 90 tire.

Lampette suggests that *Chances are the best lighting for reading in your house is in the bathroom,* in 84 pt. Gothic.

Antique Bourbon goes beyond 144 pt. in a blow-up of its label in "Antique" type.

Remington promises that *AS OF SUNDAY, OCTOBER 30,*

EVERY MAN IN AMERICA CAN SET HIS BEARD BACK 3 HOURS, in 72 pt. caps.

Tiparillo introduces Cold Smoke, a menthol-flavored cigar, in 120 pt. upper and lower case. (The cigar, incidentally, is pictured in a cake of ice.)

Quaker Oats asks *Wouldst thou believe* Quaker is America's number one cereal, hot or cold? in 72 pt., almost twice the size of *Life's* headline on the story opposite which describes New York's worst fire in the 101-year history of the city's fire department.

Fat 96 pt. Gothic is used to remind *Life's* readers that *"Us Tareyton smokers would rather fight than switch!"*

Esquire socks demands that you *GET WITH THE ACTION* in 96 pt. caps.

And so on.

Shouting type is advertising's latest fad, and one of its most annoying. It is also probably one of the least effective, because it makes what follows almost impossible to read.

It numbs the viewer as surely as if he were hit physically between the eyes.

An advertisement for the Better Vision Institute in this same issue of *Life* suggests how much better it is usually to talk softly if you really have something to say.

A handsome young woman, squinting, says *"Darling, tell me if there is anyone here I know."* In 36 pt. upper and lower case.

And it must be difficult for anyone not to read on, to be reminded that there's one (at least) at every party, blind as a bat without her glasses, squinting, straining, spoiling her good looks.

To be sure, not all advertising can be as restrained in appearance, but how pleasant it is when it is.

How much more convincing.

In the current issues of *Life* and *Look* there are thirty-one advertisements in which the headlines are set in 72 pt. type or larger. In these there are letters five inches high.

Sears and Kraft, two of the world's most successful advertisers, have double-page spreads in *Look* in which the headlines are set in similar 42 pt. characters. Obviously, these people believe it's what they have to say that counts; not how loud they can say it.

December 30

Tomorrow ends the twenty-fourth year in what I hope will be a long, happy life for Foote, Cone & Belding.

The substance in my hope is my conviction that the new corporate heads, the new general manager in Chicago, and the new chairman of the International Committee, all of whom take on their added responsibilities at a time when their predecessors still are active members of the firm, give it an unusual feeling of stability.

The company was years in recovering from the unplanned retirement of Emerson Foote, after a lengthy illness, in 1950. And while Don Belding had long said that he would retire when he was 60 years old, no one dreamed that he would make this official on his sixtieth birthday, in January, 1957. The shock was distinct and the earth rocked for months in Los Angeles.

Now, as you know, Mr. Carney and Mr. Taylor and I have taken all the necessary steps to make the succession to our various positions in the corporate structure, orderly and smooth.

And we have been able to do this with young men who are part of a remarkable record.

1967

June 12

One of our girls won a big one yesterday in Houston.

The award was the citation as Advertising Woman of the Year. It was made by the American Advertising Federation, the largest of all our industry groups—since the A.A.F. represents the total membership of all the advertising clubs in the country.

The award this year was to Shirley Polykoff, whose advertising for Clairol constitutes a classic continuing campaign that now is in its 12th year, piling success upon success.

In accepting the award, Shirley Polykoff scored several direct hits on the foolishness that infects advertising today.

"I am not," she said, "a part of the new swinging school of the kook and the young Turk. I simply don't believe that any ad is okay just because it stops the consumer, shocks the consumer or entertains him so that he falls on the floor laughing.

"Too often, ad writers write just to show off to other advertisers. It's like a closed circle with the consumer outside.

"Or as *The New Yorker* (February 18) put it, 'The audience becomes the consumer not of the products advertised but of the advertisements themselves'."

I hope Shirley's audience in Houston was listening carefully.

And that they tied what she had to say with what her own success has proved: that an advertisement is only as good as the legitimate promise it makes and the acceptance of that promise and the action that results from it.

When Shirley Polykoff began writing Clairol advertising, something less than 7% of U. S. women used hair coloring. Today the percentage has increased almost ten-fold; and Clairol is far out in front as the industry leader.

I think what I like most about the Clairol success is the fact that using Clairol products has helped so many women to look the way *they* want to, and not merely the way some unplanned genetic combination turned out.

Shirley Polykoff's has been an exciting undertaking.

September 20

There is a section in the current issue (September 18) of *Advertising Age* that should be required reading for critics of the economics of advertising who are tempted to break into print.

The cost of manufacturers' advertising is something they hold to be reckless and irresponsible, and the impression is inescapable that this is a major element in the high cost of living.

Here, from *Advertising Age,* are some facts.

The cost of advertising involved in a bottle of Coca-Cola or Pepsi-Cola or Royal Crown Cola or Hires Root Beer or Seven-Up, is only a little more than .006 cents. There is no coin small enough to represent the saving were advertising to be eliminated. Canned and frozen foods have to cost thirty-five cents before the advertising equals one cent.

You would have to buy two or three boxes of Kleenex before Kimberly-Clark could generate the first cent for advertising.

In clothing, the percentage ranges from .0011 for men's and boys' to .0084 for women's, children's and infants' clothes. Thus, a man who pays five dollars for a shirt may be paying as much as five cents for advertising. A woman who pays $49 for a dress may absorb an advertising cost of forty-one cents.

A thirty-five cent bottle of beer might cost two cents less were there no advertising to support sales. But neither magazines nor newspapers could be purchased for less for, again, there is no coin small enough to represent the savings on single copy sales were all advertising costs eliminated.

Even on a $3,000 automobile the cost of advertising is only about eighteen dollars.

The figures are from the Bureau of Internal Revenue, 1964-65. I doubt if they changed significantly last year.

October 10

One thing you can depend on in the advertising business is that it will fall all over itself attempting to climb on some shiny new bandwagon every few years.

Sometimes the wagon is filled with esoteric and exotic research leaning more and more on Freud and Adler and Jung. Sometimes it is conceived with brilliant new merchandising techniques—as when suddenly all ten-cent coupons become 7-cent coupons! Again, it will be the face of advertising that must be remodelled until all the entries in each category look exactly alike. Remember the cake mixes?

1967, I should say, is the year of the discovery of youth.

What is youth?

Youth is riding tandem on a Honda motorcycle or walking the streets with a transistor radio. Youth is playing a guitar, drinking Coke, eating pizza. Youth is long hair and mini-skirts, white lipstick and Clearasil.

Youth is a wonderful time to be alive.

Also, for the caterers of the above, and such incidental items as portable phonographs and records, panty stockings, false eyelashes, dark glasses, sandals, sarapes, and the paperback editions of the great authors—including William Burroughs—it is very good business.

Nevertheless, the size of the youth market can be misleading. The word is out that "soon half of the U. S. population will be under 25 years old," and so it will—almost (47.5%). But, as Cornelius DuBois has pointed out, "only 6.1% of family heads in the U. S. were under age 25 in 1965, a percentage that may increase to as high as 8% by 1980."

Just so, the heads of the vast majority of families who obviously buy most of the food, drugs, cosmetics, clothes, television sets, household appliances, automobiles, transportation, and conveniences of all kinds, are *more* than 25 years of age. Of the population aged 14 and over, the median age is 39.2.

Perhaps the most important thing to remember about this is that these people are apt to be serious about their purchases (the high cost of living is one reason) and foolish advertising is unlikely to move them. Advertising that is made to be taken with a youthful giggle could prove to be bitter medicine in the total mix.

1968

April 10

Twenty-five years ago, when Foote, Cone & Belding was new and small, it was possible for all of the creative people to meet together in one room, and frequently.

Right here I should say that by creative people I mean all those who have anything at all to do with the planning, preparation, circulation and research that relates to the purpose of our production, and certainly this includes our management supervisors and account executives who must interpret our clients' problems to our writers and our artists and our broadcast directors, and present the solutions that are arrived at together.

When our growth made it physically impossible to hold those meetings, I undertook to reduce what I had to say to writing; and what I had to say in some hundreds of memos was mostly about advertising (ours and that of other people, good and bad by my lights) and just about anything else that might have occurred to me to say to anyone who dropped into my office.

This was my only frequent contact with several hundred of our people, and I received numerous replies—some agreeing with my points of view, some disagreeing sharply; some forcing me to back down. Sometimes, the dialogue would be pretty one-sided for a period of weeks, then I would run head-on into controversy, or find that I had struck a warm view of concurrence.

Well, it is the point of this memo to say that once again I

have some things to say that I would like to discuss quietly in my office. But this is impossible.

You are going to have to read me.

*

I am aware of a growing concern over the relative standing of Foote, Cone & Belding as a "creative" advertising agency, according to the results of various industry contests and awards.

The most recent of these were the awards of the Advertising Club of New York, in which Foote, Cone & Belding failed to place, and I would like to comment on this.

Advertising is a business. It is not a profession and it is not an art. To be sure, it has professional overtones and it makes use of several of the arts. Nevertheless, it is a business first, last and always, and its sole purpose is to substitute for personal salesmanship. How well advertising helps to sell the products and the services with which it is concerned is the only reasonable measure of its value.

Unfortunately, this is a measure that is rarely available to awards juries. Even when it is they are prone to overlook it. Extremely successful long-time campaigns are passed over simply because they are not new. Advertisements that are filled with information, like so many advertisements for food, are rarely chosen, while advertisements that only attract attention carry off the prizes.

The current Hertz campaign, that has nothing to do with Hertz cars, is a typical example. Another, and even sadder one, was the award made last week in New York to the agency for Gablinger beer.

Shortly after Gablinger was made to cease and desist from its claim that the beer was non-fattening, which was pure advertising invention, the prize-winning agency was discharged. A $6 million campaign had resulted in the sale of only 218,000 barrels of the questionable brew.

The prize-winning campaign had cost $27 per barrel against an industry average of about $2.50.

*

Awards are pretty things with which to decorate a wall.

However, I would a good deal rather have the satisfaction of knowing that Clairol, Contac, Dial soap, Dole pineapple, Hallmark cards, Klear, Raid, Off!, Kleenex, Kotex, Kraft dinners,

Sunkist oranges and a dozen other products with whose advertising we are concerned, stand firmly in first place in their various sales categories.

This, it seems to me, is the ultimate reward.

1969

March 11

When the story of advertising in the 1960's is written by some future historian, I have an idea that the off-beat exercises that have captured the fancy of so many of our contemporaries will rate little more than a footnote.

This isn't the first time that people in the trade, on one side or the other of the advertisers' desk, have gone off on a tangent that has made everything else seem pale and old-fashioned for a time. Just prior to World War II, the advertisers of premiums all but crowded out any news of the products to which the premiums were attached; tooth paste was advertised in terms of the nail brush or something that came free with a tube, and no leading ready-to-eat cereal was packed without a toy in the box.

After the war, contests took over, and it was a thin issue of *Life* that didn't promote four or five of these.

At about the same time a couple of nondescript brothers named Townsend, spawned in some backwoods bramble, appeared on the scene with a secret check list of twenty-seven points by which they undertook to judge and amend the agencies' work for their clients, and thereby guarantee success.

The most interesting (and most exasperating) aspect of the brothers' operation was that the agencies were not allowed to see the magic 27 points, but only the results of the Townsends' analysis!

This couldn't last long. And it didn't. But the idea that there was an area of occult truths that were beyond the ability of the advertising people to cope with, fascinated a number of upper level management people to whom advertising was, indeed, a mystery, and they turned to a new set of gurus for guidance.

I am sure that my old friends and sparring partners, Ernest Dichter and Alfred Politz, would scoff at the idea, but I am convinced that Vance Packard had a good deal to do with this. *The*

Hidden Persuaders, which he wrote with a steaming pen, was all the proof many of the management people needed to be sure that advertising was, after all, a matter of conjuration; and Dichter and Politz were just the men to explain the sorcery.

But their day, too, passed by.

Now we have a new thing. A kind of non-advertising that ranges from pure fun and frolic to printed advertisements and filmed commercials that almost defy understanding.

One example of the first of these is a Ford Cortina page in this week's *Life* magazine that is headlined "Cuter'n a bug's rear"; for another, I could hardly do better (or worse) than a page in the current *New Yorker* that insists "Metaxa makes a miserable martini". If you have time you can learn that the Cortina has 21 cubic feet of trunk space; and that Metaxa tastes anything but miserable in a Manhattan. But both these pieces of information are carefully obscured.

In so far as television is concerned, the total foolishness is slightly less, because product and promise usually emerge finally and stand alone.

*

When the future historian gets around to these years, I think he may conclude that the most notable advertising of the period is the no-nonsense magazine and television advertising of Sears, Roebuck and Company.

It is apparent already, of course, that this is the most comprehensive program ever undertaken by a retailer, with separate campaigns for men's, women's and children's clothing, carpeting, major appliances, television instruments, sporting goods, power tools, batteries, tires, and so on — even including precious stones!

Half a dozen agencies are engaged in the project, and there is no single format in either print or broadcasting.

However, there is a remarkable consistency in Sears' approach to its public that is characterized by straight talk and *all* the important facts of the matter, whether this be the wearability of a pair of boys' pants or Sears' explicit guarantee in the case of batteries or tires. Everything that is pertinent is there, and it is clear.

It also is beautifully mounted.

No one but Sears, of course, will ever know exactly what the results of this advertising are. But it will be an extremely

insensitive advertiser who fails to be impressed by the direct
approaches that the world's most successful merchant is making
to the markets they both vie for.

April 22

It was Spinoza who said, "All things excellent are as difficult
as they are rare," and I urge our creative people to take this
to heart.

I assure you that it is not with the idea of pulling intellectual rank on anyone that I quote a Portuguese metaphysicist.
The fact is, I haven't thought of Spinoza since I took Philosophy
IV at the University of California, at Berkeley, some time
around 1923, in my sophomore or junior year.

The quotation happens to be something that I came across
in an article in the Ford Foundation Annual Report for 1968;
and I think it applies to our efforts, being as they must be, much
more mental than mechanical and, in every case, imaginative
rather than imitative. A great deal of advertising that is effective, including some of our own, is only good advertising. It falls
short of excellence.

What I am afraid of is that we may sometimes be too easily
satisfied — because of the exigencies of time, or simply because
our client is. In either case our work is not put to the most critical tests we can give it at every step in the production process.
Thoughts are not carefully connected to make a solid chain of
arguments or promises in printed advertisements. Television
films fail to carry out the full intent of the storyboards, and the
commercials that result are only slightly above the common-
place.

Such is the power of even poor advertising in a market of
200 million people, some of whom are bound to be interested in
almost anything (including the latest variations of bingo offered
by the foolish gasoline marketers) that it is probably hard to
come up with a flat failure.

This, however, is no excuse for dodging the difficulties that
are involved in the pursuit of excellence. One of these is to hold
up first efforts to the severest scrutiny no matter how good they
look, to seek alternatives and compare these honestly.

This, I believe, is the first step toward excellence in our business. Quick and easy satisfaction is a step toward mediocrity.

July 24

I am afraid that an increasing number of advertisers are going headlong down a primrose path, and I trust that we will use all our ingenuity to hold our clients back.

The path to which I refer is decorated with psychedelic drawings in the Andy Warhol-Peter Max manner, and while these may be fine as art, although I question this, I am sure they fail to say anything either intelligent or intelligible insofar as advertising is concerned. They are part of a game.

Games take time to play.

And, unfortunately, people don't spend time on advertising — except on television advertising from which they can't escape — except to find out something, which is very nearly impossible in the Warhol-Max school, where substance gives way entirely to technique.

Anyway, the point I want to make is that we shouldn't pay too much attention to the fun-people on parade on Michigan Avenue, without following them also into the nearest Walgreen drug store or Jewel or A&P supermarket to see how serious they suddenly become when it comes to spending money.

It is this mood to which our advertising should be addressed.

This doesn't mean that it has to be pedestrian. It only means that it ought to be clear what we are trying to say.

Up to now it usually has been.

I hope we'll keep this up. And not follow American Oil, Sunshine Biscuit, 7-Up, and some of the others who appear to be caught up in the psychedelic foolishness.

Epilogue — 1972

Looking back over forty-odd years in advertising I find it greatly changed or, perhaps I should say, much more sophisticated. Both the change and the sophistication began with radio and speeded up with the introduction of television at the close of World War II.

Before the days of radio and the dependence of advertisers and their agencies on statistics ground out by a number of independent operators to indicate the popularity, and the resulting circulation of programs, advertising was a very personal business. Actually, the magazines and newspapers had their statistics, too, but the vital decisions on publication schedules were made most often by the advertisers' top men (frequently the president or chairman of the company or some long-time legendary advertising manager) and a group of the most talented and persuasive salesmen ever to represent an industry.

Corporate and agency doors opened wide and the red carpet was forever rolled out for men like Fred Healy of Curtis (*Saturday Evening Post* and *Ladies' Home Journal*); for Lee Brantley and Arthur H. (Red) Motley of Crowell-Collier, and subsequently, *Parade;* and John Sterling of *McCall's* and, later, *This Week.* Mortimer Berkowitz represented Hearst's *American Weekly* in the owner's own rich style; and C. D. Jackson stood on his head in my living room to amuse my small daughter and, incidentally, regale me with success stories from *Life.*

No longer are any but occasional sales made of radio or television time or publication or outdoor space. All these are bought by slide rule and survey from very nearly faceless salesmen, who merely deliver the mathematical and research results which then are processed by business school graduates who deal solely in decimals and demographics.

The only thing wrong with this is that the new way, while not nearly so much fun as the old one, produces far better results.

Otherwise, the principal change in advertising during these forty years, and culminating in the present consumer restlessness, has been in a manufactured public dissatisfaction with it. What once was a question of ethics now is becoming one of morals. Criticism of advertising that was formerly a question of honesty now is a matter of philosophy. The question of how to advertise is being superseded by the question of whether to advertise. And the answer should not be written by Ralph Nader or any of his legions.

Advertising is a poor subject about which to generalize. Nevertheless, most of the opinions people hold about it and most of the judgments that are made about it are generalizations — nearly all just now in the negative.

This is foolish and unwarranted, and when I hear advertising ridiculed and lambasted as a social and moral problem, I find it hard to wait my turn to dissent. Sometimes this is a long wait, too, because it is fashionable to attack advertising and to exaggerate its influence and its effect with any number of examples. While most of these are drawn from television, they are made to apply to all advertising, and this is where my rebuttal begins.

First, though, let me say that there is a good deal of advertising that I find tasteless, rude (interruptive) and overstated; also painfully insistent and agonizingly repetitious. Television has accentuated all this. It is easy to overlook a magazine or newspaper advertisement or even the enormous volume of direct mail, that is of no personal interest. It is almost impossible to ignore a television advertisement that interrupts any program to which one is tuned. Just so, most of the criticism of advertising turns out to be criticism of television advertising.

With much if not most of the argument I agree, as long as it is confined to broadcasting. Otherwise, I enter into rebuttal one of the largest classifications in the entire industry, which is retailers' advertising, appearing primarily in newspapers, and rarely, if ever, attacked. This, I suppose, is because the advertising of department stores and specialty shops and the food chains is accepted without thinking as hard core news about products and prices. The manufacturers' advertising, which crowds the airwaves, is the base upon which much of the retailers' advertising rests without objection.

During the seven hours each day that the average television set is turned on there is an outpouring of commercial announcements only a small percentage of which can possibly be of immediate interest to any given viewer. If one has developed a headache or is suffering from indigestion or problems in the bathroom or the laundry, or with feeding a bored husband or balky children dissatisfied with their breakfast, say, then a television advertisement may make a welcome suggestion. But if none of these things pertains, and advertising merely interrupts the entertainment (such as it is, particularly in the daytime) then advertising may be an annoyance.

This is something that will require the best thinking of the best brains in the industry to ameliorate. There are many questions to be resolved. Should the commercials be bunched and run between programs, as in Europe? Should the clutter of 10, 20 and 30-second commercials be reduced by accommodating only a limited number of products during a commercial period?

Or should there be any commercials at all, with license fees applied to pay the broadcasting bill?

Akin to judging all advertising in terms of television (and outdoor advertising to which I shall return, since it comes under similar castigation) is the habit of the severest critics to link television advertising and television programming as equally the responsibility of the advertisers. The truth is that the broadcasters, both networks and independent station owners, are exclusively responsible. Years ago radio programming got out of the hands of the broadcasters. Television started out the same way. But the owners and operators had had enough of that and soon established their own control. Today, they, and they alone in the industry, choose programs.

To be sure, these are chosen to meet, and hopefully to beat, competition, so that the networks or the stations involved can offer the most audience per dollar to advertisers. But the advertiser's choice is only to contract or not to contract for whatever time and talent the broadcasters offer.

Advertising has always been subject to criticism in general terms for offenses that are particular. I suppose this will always be so. Certainly it is true in the case of television. Young girls who find romance in a bottle of mouth wash, grown women who go into ecstasy over cleansers and washing powders, and men whose failing marriages are saved through their wives' discovery of a better tasting coffee, represent the dregs of advertising creativity. This is not so much dishonest as it is licensed and, I suppose, harmless, exaggeration.

The real trouble lies in the continuous interruption and the low level of interest of so many of the subjects (products) involved, and the industry has yet to come up with a way out of what is everyone's dilemma. I say everyone's because the public is not about to give up the programming that is free, and pay television is the only alternative. I expect there will eventually be pay television, with instruments metered to receive select programming. But this will go side by side with advertiser-paid-for television because most set owners are known to feel that viewing the commercials is a fair price to pay for the news and the entertainment that arrives via the tube.

I continue to think, after twenty-five years of gross dissatisfaction with much that appears on the television screen, that the vast majority of viewers are getting what they want. It is I who am out of step. However, there are beginning to be more and more serious broadcasts, of news and opinion, and programs that picture and discuss important subjects in detail and in depth for limited audiences.

The truth of the matter is, if one looks carefully at the television listings in newspapers, or in *TV Guide,* and chooses wisely, television can be very rewarding. If its news programs are mostly only headlines and pictures, the pictures are often worth a good many words, and the result is a deep and lasting impression.

No medium as powerful as television can forever escape its obligations, and television gives ample evidence that at least some of the broadcasters know this. Recently, as James Reston has pointed out in *The New York Times,* "we have seen the possibilities of television as a great unifying force in the nation as we have together viewed the details of a Presidential election; the death of two former Presidents of the United States; the bombings of Hanoi; the inauguration of President Nixon; the announcement of the cease-fire in Viet Nam; and, finally, the burial ceremony of President Johnson."

These were great moments and television etched them in millions of minds as no other medium could. The vital problem with television is not in its coverage of historic events, but in its development of important programs of its own in the absence of dramatic happenings outside. That these important programs should include entertainment is part of the problem and part of the promise.

One can only hope that the advertising on these more serious or more imaginative programs will follow suit. Meanwhile, advertising will be judged by the literate and articulate public on the basis of the extravagance and the ubiquity that are held to be its hallmarks.

Since there is little likelihood that television will ever be able to accommodate small, special interest programs in the way a growing list of medium-size magazines do, I think the total magazine concept for television (as I have discussed this on so many previous occasions) offers the only means of programming for everyone. The latest Nielsen Report shows 20 million households tuned in to "All in the Family," the top-rated program in a typical week, and 25 million tuned to the two competing network shows, leaving more than half of U. S. families as a potential for something quite different from situation comedy and cops and robbers—if only it isn't necessary to attract them all.

My solution continues to be to package large audience programs with limited interest programs, all of the broadcasters' choosing, and offer these to advertisers at an average audience rate, in order to force advertiser support for a limited number of cultural, artistic or educational programs, and the broadcasting of controversial points of view on matters of public concern.

* * *

Hardly less blatant than much of television advertising is what is known in the trade as outdoor, which includes painted signs, posters and advertising on walls. Government regulations have kept the painted bulletins and other signs off federally financed turnpikes and thruways, and the outdoor advertising companies have been increasingly kind to the countryside.

On the other hand, small business interests, frequently posting homemade designs, together with a coterie of callous large advertisers, make the approach to almost every village in the land a passage through a maze of ugly signs. Behind and above these, gasoline filling stations raise their beckoning emblems into the sky, and when you reach the cities there is almost no space not occupied by a building that isn't decorated with billboards, frequently rising above still other billboards. Together, with signs painted on the side of dilapidated buildings, this is advertising's greatest aesthetic assault.

* * *

I have barely mentioned direct mail advertising. Nor shall I go any farther than to point out that the increasing volume through the years has made it an increasing nuisance to many people. Still, it is easily got rid of if the subject is of no interest. Relief is as close as the nearest wastebasket or garbage can. But this is only one side of the picture. It is part of the value of direct mail advertising that it provides ample space to tell a complete story and to illustrate this copiously. If the subject is appealing, direct advertising usually tells you all you want to know about it.

If you consider the catalogues and flyers sent out to selected prospects by the mail order companies and specialty manufacturers as aids to shopping at home, which they are, direct mail advertising can be a boon.

* * *

I have said that the most significant change in advertising in recent years has been in the public attitude toward it. But this may be exaggerated.

I am not entirely persuaded that polls of public opinion represent anything more than a reflection of the deponents' most recent unpleasant experience with advertising dredged up, as it were, by the interviewers' slanted questioning. To put this another way, I believe most advertising is accepted or rejected unemotionally and without reflection until and unless deep probing finds a sore spot.

The concern of most people with advertising must be with its usefulness, with what it tells them of importance and whether it tells the truth. Otherwise, unless they are prompted, they could hardly care less about its moral implications. These are the concern of the critics of our society who really don't like anything about it the way it is. Since advertising touches almost every one of us almost every day, and since some of this contact is bound to be abrasive, if only because of what seems to be needless repetition, advertising is the fairest of game for both professional and amateur reformers.

The moral, or social criticisms are well established, and constantly repeated in the unequivocal terms of a manifesto.

The first insistence is that advertising leads people to buy things they do not need, and the second is that it does this by some kind of mesmerism, some kind of diabolic direction of which the millions of subjects are unaware. With the first of these I agree heartily: advertising does most certainly encourage people to buy things that are in no way necessities, but this is surely the result of civilization itself and the discoveries of imaginative men.

To begin with you may consider the invention of the wheel. Nobody needed it; the backs of men were plenty strong. Or take music. Or books. Or shoes. And then consider the labor force. How is it to be employed if we were to eliminate the manufacture of such non-essentials as automobiles, radio and television sets, electric stoves and gas furnaces, soaps and cleansers, cosmetics for women and shaving instruments and wild sports shirts for men, and the thousand and one prepared (and enriched) food products, that raise our living standard above merely subsistence?

And if we are to catalog and legislate essential and non-essential articles and categories, who is to make the determinations? This is a question that neither Dr. Toynbee, the historian and philosopher, nor John Kenneth Galbraith, the economist, nor Mrs. Virginia Knauer, President Nixon's advisor on consumer affairs, has undertaken to answer. Were it not that these are established authorities, their charges of uneconomic and immoral manipulation through advertising could be ignored. Admitting that advertising does, indeed, induce people to buy many things for which they have no vital need, but which they want for various reasons that have nothing whatever to do with advertising, the charge of persuasion by means of psychological or occult misbehavior is too ridiculous to dwell on. To be sure, advertising uses many of the devices of the live salesman. But the public can always ignore these.

The American economic system and the advertising that supports it are both based on the integrity of the basic business community and its satellites. One would be extremely foolish to maintain that all businesses are honest and all advertising above board. They are not. But it is the rare miscreant who is not caught up quickly by the very public that he has sought to defraud.

It is the inexorable right of this public not to buy anything a second time that has failed it the first. The promises that advertising makes are made in the open and they cannot be broken in secret.

Since advertising is something anyone can do, it is subject to wild lapses of taste and intellect, particularly in television where its reach is longest. But just as most business people know that honest advertising puts their promises on the line, good taste and greater artistry in television commercials may not be far behind. If television programming follows suit, away from the insipid sitcoms and the blood and thunder that are so large a part of the total picture, criticism of advertising will become a good deal less inclusive.

Fairfax M. Cone